PAT STANTON'S HIBERNIAN DREAM TEAM

Pat Stanton is one of Hibernian Football Club's greatest ever players. He made his debut for Hibs in 1963 and served the club with distinction for thirteen years. During that time, Pat captained Hibs to three major trophies. Easter Road has always been Pat's spiritual home and he continues to appear there as a match day host. Pat also works for the Scottish Premier League. Although it is over thirty years since he played his last game for Hibernian, Pat Stanton is still revered by the club's supporters.

Ted Brack is a retired head teacher and lifelong Hibs supporter. Ted's book *There is a Bonny Fitba Team*, which chronicled half a century of supporting Hibernian Football Club, reached number five in the Scottish Book Charts in June 2009.

Also by Ted Brack
There is a Bonny Fitba Team: Fifty Years on the Hibee Highway

PAT STANTON'S HIBERNIAN DREAM TEAM

Pat Stanton

with Ted Brack

BLACK & WHITE PUBLISHING

First published 2010
by Black & White Publishing Ltd
29 Ocean Drive, Edinburgh EH6 6JL

1 3 5 7 9 10 8 6 4 2   10 11 12 13

ISBN: 978 1 84502 287 7

Copyright © Ted Brack and Pat Stanton 2010

Typeset by Ellipsis Books Limited, Glasgow
Printed and bound by MPG Books Ltd, Bodmin

CONTENTS

ACKNOWLEDGEMENTS

Everyone who knows me knows how much I love Hibernian Football Club. Writing this book has been a pleasure. I have remembered great players and great matches and recalled many happy memories.

I would like to thank all the outstanding players I have played with and all the managers I have played under for sharing my Hibernian career with me. I would also like to thank the magnificent Hibs players I have watched as a supporter before I signed on at Easter Road and after I retired. It has been a joy to watch you all strutting your stuff.

Finally, I would like to thank my co-author Ted Brack. We had some terrific discussions as I trawled the archives of my mind to compare and contrast the many gifted Hibees who have graced Easter Road during my lifetime. Ted has managed to write down what we talked about in a manner that I think is completely accurate and readable. I thank him for that.

Pat Stanton

As I stood on the old Easter Road terracing back in the seventies and thrilled to the exciting, classic football served up by Turnbull's Tornadoes, I marvelled at the play of Pat Stanton. Here was a man who had all the footballing skills, which he displayed in the most elegant, stylish manner. Pat wasn't just an exceptional player though; he was a Hibs supporter in a jersey. His affection for our great club matched that of all of us in the crowd. This made Pat even more special in our eyes.

I never dreamt that nearly forty years later I would be sitting with Pat at my dining room table debating the merits of Hibs' greatest players over a cup of tea. What came through to me in our discussions was Pat's knowledge of football. He knows the game inside out and is full of wisdom and insight when discussing players and matches. Pat had a host of memories and stories to share and he delivered them all in his own unassuming and wryly humorous style.

What shone through most of all was Pat's deep love for Hibernian Football Club. Pat has the same esteem for our team as we supporters have for him. It was an honour and a privilege for me to collaborate with Pat on the writing of this book.

Pat, thank you very much for giving me the opportunity to do so.

Ted Brack

We would both like to thank everyone at Black & White Publishing for their help and support in producing this book.

FOREWORD
By Sir Alex Ferguson

When asked to do a foreword for this book on the best of Hibs teams or players, I thought to myself, 'Now there's a challenge.' How could you sift through the galaxy of great players who wore the famous green and white and come up with a definitive selection? Well, you could if you were Pat Stanton, as it requires someone old enough (dare I say that) to search the inner reaches of his memory to the era when I, as a young boy, watched that famous Hibs team of the early fifties destroy my boyhood heroes, Rangers, at Ibrox Park. I thought to myself, 'That's nae fair,' doing that to the Rangers.

Smith, Johnstone, Reilly, Turnbull and Ormond are etched in my mind forever and everyone else's who is old enough to have seen them play. As time went on and I became a player myself, I played against Pat many times and even from an early age you could see he was destined to become one of the greats. Pat was there to testify to the brilliance of that great team of the seventies. Blackley, Cormack, O'Rourke, Gordon and, of course, Pat himself. One question: if John Brownlie hadn't broken his leg, how good would he have become? Well, only Pat Stanton could answer that.

I look forward to reading this attempt to unravel the pecking order of greatness of these legends in Hibs history: Joe Baker, Pat Quinn, Willie Hamilton, Tommy Younger – you could go on and on and it would be absolutely riveting to analyse and read. Just please don't leave out big John McNamee – I've still got his stud marks on the back of my head!

It is a pleasure to contribute to this exciting book by a great friend and colleague.

Alex. Ferguson

FOREWORD
By Grant Stott

As someone whose footballing prowess was limited to one solitary appearance in goals for James Gillespie's High School in a match against Liberton High School back in 1983, and whose only touch in the game was fluffing a ball into the net (giving Libby High their only goal in a 7-1 win), you may well be wondering why on earth I was asked to provide a foreword to a book by Pat Stanton.

To be honest, so am I, but I cannot think of any bigger thrill for a Hibs fan – other than playing for our team perhaps – than to be asked to contribute to a book by the one and only Pat Stanton!! Safe to say, I didn't need asking twice. I said yes quicker than Hibs did when they accepted that offer from Hearts for Brian Hamilton.

For nearly ten years, I have worked alongside Pat at Easter Road as Corporate Hospitality host on match days which, let's face it, isn't exactly the toughest gig in the world for a Hibee. Watching the games and interviewing many of the players is a dream job, no question, but without doubt, the most exciting aspect was being introduced to, and in turn becoming friends with, three legendary former players who hosted tables: Pat Stanton, Lawrie Reilly and, until his untimely death in 2003, Joe Baker.

Getting to know and sitting beside these men on match days is the stuff that dreams are made of – not least for my

Dad, Les, who Pat regularly slags off about his bunnet and who Lawrie, despite being more than ten years his senior, refers to as 'Dad'.

To get to know The Quiet Man over the years has been, quite simply, a delight and an honour. The Stott's have supported Hibs for generations. My Grandad, Jackie Stott, who grew up on the other side of the bridge from Easter Road Stadium in Bothwell Street in the 1920s, supported Hibs as both man and boy which, in turn, led to my father following faithfully – even though he was to be brought up in deepest, darkest Dalry. By the time it came to my big brother John and I, there really was no other choice.

The name Pat Stanton is one I've grown up with. In fact, when I was growing up I saw him every day – first thing in the morning and last thing at night. Reason being his face adorned the wall of the bedroom I shared with my brother, as it was slap bang in the middle of that iconic Edinburgh Evening News commemorative poster from Hibs' triumphs in the League and Drybrough Cups in 1972; the very same poster forever immortalised in *Trainspotting*.

However, back then, as a wee seven- or eight-year-old boy, I wasn't a Hibs fan. It was my brother who was (and still is) into all things Hibs; quite simply he lived and breathed them.

So, as wee brothers do, I rebelled against this and showed no interest at all. But despite my apparent ignorance, I couldn't help but soak up so much about the club, such was John's enthusiasm.

Without ever having seen Hibs play, I knew all about Stanton, O'Rourke, Cropley, Edwards, the late Alan Gordon et al. Turnbull's Tornadoes was a tune I knew word for word and I had no choice in this as it was on the record player turntable in our bedroom about every five minutes.

Thankfully, my rebellion didn't last and, in time, I saw the light and started going to the games with my Dad but by then, regrettably for me, Pat's playing days were over. I'd missed my chance to see him in action. But since I have been going to watch Hibs play, I've seen some great (and some not so great) players grace the hallowed turf at Easter Road.

Some were always destined to play at the highest level, like John Collins and Andy Goram who went on to play for Scotland back in the good old days when Scotland qualified for things. Others could do no wrong in my eyes, like Keith, Keith, Keith, Keith Wright and one of my all time favourites, Kevin McAllister, who was just a joy to watch.

Of the hundreds of football clubs he has played for, I think Hibs got the very best out of Darren Jackson when he was at Easter Road and, without question, one of the most brilliantly bonkers players ever to entertain us between the sticks was John Burridge.

We've had stars like Franck Sauzée and Russell Latapy exciting us with their skill and in more recent times I've 'oohed' and 'aahed' like a girl at the sight of David Murphy on the ball.

Of the more recent young guns, one player who stands out for me during his time at Hibs was Scott Brown, a player who was just the right side of radge . . . most of the time.

But could I come up with an all time dream team? Players, subs, managers, the lot? To be honest, I don't think I'm in any way near qualified.

But I know a man who is.

Pat Stanton has regaled me with many tales on match days of his time as a supporter, player and manager, and they were always entertaining, sometimes fascinating and often down-right unbelievable – and I don't just mean the stories of his trips abroad when he roomed with Jimmy O'Rourke!!

I never tire of hearing him tell the story of how he sat in

the changing room, marvelling at the sight of the very stylish Baker boy in his linen suit on his return to Hibs in the late 60s – a tale that you can read in full later in this book.

Pat's dry sense of humour when dealing with officials has had me in stitches and I've sat enthralled hearing about his run-ins with Eddie Turnbull – run-ins which led to tensions between the two that still exist to this day.

Since he made his Hibs debut as a player in 1963, Pat has been in and around our great club in one capacity or another for nearly forty years and has followed the team for even longer, so I can't think of anyone more suitably qualified than Pat Stanton to write a book such as this.

You may not agree with all his choices but given his pedigree and his knowledge of all things Hibs, it is certain that this book will be an absolutely fascinating read and an open and honest insight for all Hibs fans from a man who knows more than most.

Glory, and indeed, Glory.

Grant Stott

INTRODUCTION

My great, great, great, grand uncle Michael Whelehan was the co-founder of Hibernian Football Club and the first captain of our great team. I played for Hibs for thirteen years and captained the club to three trophies. I played 680 games for the Hibees and scored eighty-three goals. When my playing career came to an end, I was privileged to become manager of Hibernian. Before and after my official involvement with Hibs, I have been a faithful supporter of what I consider to be one of Scotland's greatest and most romantic football teams. Hibs are literally in my blood. If you cut me, I would probably bleed green with white sleeves.

I am going to surprise a lot of people right at the start of this book by revealing that I almost never signed for Hibs at all. As a teenager, I used to train at Easter Road and I was absolutely delighted when Hibs asked me to sign provisional forms. I didn't waste any time in signing on the dotted line. These were forms that tied you to a club until you were old enough to sign as a professional. In those days, it was very rare for a youngster, having signed provisional forms with one club, to end up signing professional forms with another club.

As time went on, Hibs gave no indication of wanting to sign me on a full contract and I became increasingly concerned and disappointed. Other clubs, including Chelsea, were starting to show an interest in me and although Hibs was the team I wanted, I was beginning to wonder if they wanted me.

My mother telephoned the SFA to ask what the situation was with my provisional contract. To our amazement she was told that no provisional forms had been registered in my name. When we made further enquiries, we discovered that the club had put my forms away in a drawer. This gave them the chance to take their time before making a final decision. If they decided in due course that I was definitely worth signing, they could then register me and submit my forms. If they were of the opinion that I wasn't good enough then they could just tear the forms up.

We were furious and hurt. Hibs, on hearing of the interest of other clubs, somewhat belatedly began to display a sense of urgency. My dad and I felt so strongly that we made them sweat before I agreed to a professional contract. If it had been any other club that had treated me in this way, I would have gone elsewhere on a point of principle. It wasn't any other club though; it was the Hibs, our family's team, and despite feeling my trust had been betrayed, I couldn't stop myself committing my future to the club I loved.

So began a relationship that endures to this day. On my first day of full training, one of the coaches, Jimmy McColl, said to me, 'Remember Pat son, loyalty only works one way in this business. No matter how loyal you are to a club, they will get rid of you when they think the time is right.' That wasn't what I wanted to hear on my first day as a fully fledged Hibs player but Jimmy was right. Thirteen years later I was to leave the club in circumstances that were not of my choosing. In the process of doing so, I was treated very poorly by my then manager, Eddie Turnbull. I will reveal the full story of that episode later in this book.

At the time I joined Hibs, the club used to hold a public

trial at the start of the new season. The first team would play the reserves and this match gave the supporters the chance to take an initial look at any new signings. When I turned up for this match, I was told to go through to the away dressing room and join the reserve squad. That was what I had expected but I hadn't bargained for what happened next. One of the backroom staff handed out the eleven strips (there were no substitutes in those days) and then left the room. He hadn't given me a strip and it dawned on me that I wasn't going to take part in the trial. Looking back, that probably wasn't too surprising since I was still very much a novice. At the time though I was totally devastated. I can still remember the bitter disappointment I felt to this day.

Fourteen years later, I won the league with Celtic at Easter Road of all places. I can remember after the match sitting once again in the away dressing room at Easter Road and reflecting upon one of the high points of my career. Do you know what came into my mind as I sat there? The Monday night in August all those years ago when I had last sat in this room feeling despair at being left out of the public trial. If ever there was an example of the highs and lows of football then this was it.

So my time with Hibs didn't get off to the smoothest of starts. Very quickly though things changed for the better and I was privileged to enjoy a great career playing for and captaining the team that I loved in front of the best supporters in the world.

There were many highlights and I looked forward to every game. I used to particularly relish the derby matches with Hearts. If you weren't fully charged up in the week before one of those games then there was something wrong with you. We were always desperate to win to give our supporters the bragging rights of the city and it was really hard to take if you lost. We would console each other with platitudes like, 'Never mind, the sun will still come up tomorrow.' The problem was that you just didn't want to look at it.

One game against the Hearts that left us with nothing but joy was, of course, the famous 7–0 victory at Tynecastle in the Ne'erday derby of 1973. That was such a monumental achievement that it took a few days for it to sink in. Usually after a match, Jimmy O'Rourke, Alan Gordon and I would go for a couple of pints. Not on this occasion. We were completely drained by the magnitude of what we had just taken part in. I can remember looking round our dressing room at full time thinking just how many great players were in there with me.

I have watched and played with many outstandingly gifted Hibs players. When you support Hibs, you don't expect consistent success but you are guaranteed excitement and unpredictability. You will usually also see football played in the proper manner with the ball being kept on the grass and skill being the order of the day. That is the Hibernian way and the turf at Easter Road has been graced by a number of footballers of the highest quality, many of whom have been international class and some of whom have been, in my opinion, world class.

This book is all about my opinion. I have collaborated in producing the book with Ted Brack, author of the recent best-selling Hibs volume *There is a Bonny Fitba Team*. Ted and I go back a long way and we share a lifelong love for all things Hibernian. Something else we have in common is a date. I was born on 13 September 1944, and on that same date twenty-five years later Ted was married. As Ted and his new wife Margaret were walking down the aisle on that sunny, autumn Saturday in 1969, I was leading Hibs to a victory at Parkhead against Jock Stein's great Celtic team. It was very rare for Celtic to lose during the sixties and seventies. It was almost unheard of for them to be beaten at their fortress of a ground in Glasgow's East End. Well, that day they were well beaten by the Hibs and I even managed to score one of the goals. That is one of my many Hibernian memories and this book is full of such fond recollections.

I have been presented with the pleasant but daunting challenge of selecting my all-time great Hibernian Dream Team. In carrying out this task, I have been able to consider all the Hibee greats whom I played with and all the talented players I was able to watch representing our club before I signed for Hibs and after my playing career ended. Over the years, Hibs have fielded a galaxy of very special players and I have been fortunate enough to see many of them in action. In compiling my dream team, I have been spoiled for choice.

When I managed Hibs, the playing staff was not the strongest in the club's history and, as money was tight for the board at that time, I was never able to significantly expand my squad of players. This meant that team selection could be difficult. Some weeks, I would be scratching my head as I tried to put together a potent combination from what were, in all honesty, somewhat limited resources. In writing this book, I have had the opposite experience as I have had an embarrassment of riches to choose from.

How do you pick one goalkeeper, for example, from last lines of defence of the quality of Tommy Younger, Ronnie Simpson, Alan Rough, Andy Goram and Jim Leighton? Or what about trying to decide on two central midfield players from a stellar list which includes Bobby Johnstone, Eddie Turnbull, Pat Quinn, Willie Hamilton, Peter Cormack, Alex Edwards, Alex Cropley, Pat McGinlay, Russell Latapy and Scott Brown? Then there is centre forward. I truly believe that in my lifetime, Hibs have produced two genuinely world-class centre forwards in Lawrie Reilly and Joe Baker. To these two green and white galacticos, I can add Joe's brother Gerry, Neil Martin, Joe MacBride, the elegant, classy Alan Gordon who led the line in the Turnbull's Tornadoes team which I captained, Keith Wright the hero of Hibs 1991 League Cup triumph and the rumbustious Garry O'Connor who did such a good job in spearheading Tony Mowbray's 'Teenage Kicks' group of gifted young players.

You'll be beginning to appreciate just how many high-class performers have worn the green and white of Hibs and you'll be realising too that I have had my work cut out in choosing my team. I have also selected seven substitutes. These are players who would normally have walked into any team at any time but who have had to be content with a seat on the bench on this occasion, such has been the wonderful array of talent at my disposal. I have named a captain for my team too. We have had some great skippers over the years. In my early days of watching Hibs, the one and only Gordon Smith led the team out. Gordon passed the armband to another all-time great Hibee in Eddie Turnbull and Eddie was succeeded by such fine leaders as John Fraser, Joe Davis, George Stewart, Murdo McLeod, current manager John Hughes, Franck Sauzée and Rob Jones. I captained Hibs for many years myself, of course, and Ted has suggested that I should consider myself for inclusion in my Hibs dream team both as captain and player. I am very tempted to do so. What a pleasure it would be to play in such a team of all talents. However, part of me thinks that it would be quite good to be on the outside looking in. It would certainly be nice to sit back and watch my Dream Team in action. I'm really not sure, so I am going to think about this one and keep you in suspense until later in the book.

The choice of team manager to coach and inspire my side was crucial and again I have had a top team of tacticians to choose from. A short list which includes Hugh Shaw, Jock Stein, Bob Shankly, Eddie Turnbull, Alex Miller, Alex McLeish and Tony Mowbray is not too shabby.

I am sure that all of you who read this book will have your favourite players and your own ideas as to who should be included in my team. I know that my choices will spark a great deal of discussion and perhaps even the odd argument among fellow Hibees. Once thing is for certain, I have had great fun deciding on my final line up and what a line up it is – a Hibs team to beat the world!

I have devoted a chapter to every section of the team and in each chapter I have recalled great Hibs games and great Hibs players. I have a host of memories to share with you and a myriad of tales to tell from on the pitch and inside the dressing room. I will tell you what made certain players special and also reveal what some of these Hibee superstars were like as people.

My views will be personal, at times maybe controversial, but always honest. By the end of the book, I will be able to share with you what I think is Hibs' greatest ever team. Making my choice has been a labour of love and an absolute pleasure. I hope you enjoy reading this book as much as I have enjoyed writing it.

PAT'S STATS

AS A PLAYER

Hibernian FC (1963-1976)
> 680 appearances
> 83 goals
> 1 League Cup winners medal
> 2 Drybrough Cup winners medals

Glasgow Celtic FC (1976-1978)
> 44 appearances
> 1 Scottish League Championship winners medal
> 1 Scottish Cup winners medal

Scotland (1966-1974)
> 16 full caps (3 times as captain)
> 7 inter-league caps
> 3 under 23 caps
> 1 under 21 cap (as an over-age player)

Scotland's Player of the Year in 1970

AS A MANAGER

Aberdeen (1978-1980)
> Assistant Manager to Alex Ferguson

Cowdenbeath (1980)
> Manager

Dunfermline Athletic (1980-1982)
> Manager

Hibernian FC (1982-1984)
> Manager

1

GOALKEEPING GREATS

Every team needs a good goalkeeper. If defenders have faith in their keeper, they play with confidence and that confidence spreads through the team. The back four are more relaxed, midfield players are more inclined to attack and forwards can concentrate on their own jobs. On the other hand, if you don't trust your goalie, every outfield player becomes nervous and negative and the team tenses up. This obviously inhibits the team's ability to play with freedom.

It's essential then that you have a reliable last line of defence. If your goalkeeper is better than that and can pull off amazing saves, then he can inspire the rest of the side. Hibs have had some great goalkeepers but we have also had some, especially in recent years, who have been liabilities.

Nobody could call the first Hibs goalkeeper I saw a liability. That keeper was Tommy Younger and he was one of the very best. Tommy cut a striking figure. He was tall with blond hair and wore the bright yellow jersey which goalies favoured in the 1950s. Although he was powerfully built, big Tommy was really athletic. His agility belied his size. He was a great goalkeeper in a great team, as he played in the talented Hibs squad that won league titles and it wasn't long before he was picked for Scotland. During his Hibs career, he was called up for national service and posted to Germany. This didn't deter the big man. He came to an arrangement with his commanding officer which allowed him to work longer hours during the week to complete his army duties. In return, he was given permission to fly home to Scotland on a Friday to be available for Hibs. He travelled to and from Germany so frequently that he received an award from the airline company and earned himself the nickname of 'Tommy Offenbach'.

Tommy left Hibs to move to Liverpool. I am not sure why. At that time, Hibs were a much better team and he wouldn't have earned any extra money because the maximum wage was still in force. He also played for Leeds United during his stint down south.

The highlight of Tommy's career was when he was chosen to captain Scotland in the 1958 World Cup finals in Sweden. This was a great honour and he was rightly proud of it. When Tommy retired, he became a successful businessman and Tom Hart invited him on to the Hibs board. He was a larger than life character in more ways than one. Never a lightweight, he had gained weight from his playing days. He was also a big presence. With a cigar in one hand and a glass in the other, Tommy was great company in the board room. He represented Hibs on the SFA Executive and eventually became SFA President. By that time, the big man's health was not good and sadly, he passed away through heart problems at the age of fifty-three, just eight months into his presidency.

Hibs' next quality goalkeeper was Lawrie Leslie. Like me, Lawrie came from Niddrie. He was a top keeper and, like Tommy Younger, also played for Scotland. Mind you, Lawrie got his caps after he left Hibs. We let him go to Airdrie for a small fee. He was then signed by West Ham. I never understood why we let Lawrie go. He came back to Easter Road and played some great games against Hibs.

Lawrie was really brave. He liked nothing better than

throwing himself at an oncoming forward's feet and coming up with the ball. His courage caused him a few injuries in his time. However, one of his injuries was a stroke of good luck. He was chosen to play against England at Wembley in 1961 but had to call off through injury. I'll bet he was glad. Frank Haffey of Celtic took Lawrie's place and England won 9–3. Ever since, Haffey has been remembered for the wrong reasons and no doubt he always will be. Lawrie was well out of that one.

Lawrie's best game for Hibs was the famous 4–3 Scottish Cup win at Tynecastle in 1958. Hearts won the league that year and they had a great team. Everybody remembers this game for Joe Baker's four goals but we could easily have lost 5–4 because Hearts just kept coming at us. Lawrie was outstanding though. He pulled off some incredible saves and made a famous victory possible. At full time Lawrie was carried off a hero on the shoulders of Hibs fans who had run on to the pitch. He deserved to be because he had been truly immense.

When I started at Hibs, Ronnie Simpson was the first team goalkeeper. Ronnie was small and slight but he had massive feet! His feet were out of proportion to the rest of his body and he wasn't afraid to use them. Ronnie saved nearly as many shots with his legs and feet as he did with his hands. People used to say that he was a lucky goalkeeper but he wasn't. He used his body to make saves too often for it to be luck. Ronnie read the game really well and made sure that he got himself in the right positions. Don't get me wrong – his handling was excellent too. He was just an all round good goalie.

Ronnie gave me some really good advice when I was starting out in the Hibs' first team. I was a bit impetuous in those days and used to dive in to tackles on the edge of our own penalty area. Ronnie coached me in how to stay on my feet, read the game and judge the correct time to make my move. He told me, 'You're as much use to the team sitting in the stand as you are sitting on your backside at the edge of the box.' It was simple but effective advice and helped to make me a better defender.

Ronnie is probably best remembered now for keeping goal when Celtic won the European Cup in 1967. The man who picked him for that match and made him a Celtic regular was Jock Stein, of course. Yet the same Stein had allowed Ronnie to go to Parkhead for a nominal fee when he was manager of Hibs. People have said since then that letting Ronnie leave Hibs for Celtic was a deliberate ploy by big Jock because he knew that he would be taking over at Celtic Park sooner rather than later. I don't believe that. I suspect that Ronnie and Stein had probably had a disagreement and the Big Man decided to move Ronnie on. Ronnie was an old pro when Jock came to Easter Road as a still relatively young manager. He probably didn't make things easy for his new boss so Stein moved him out. When he came back to Celtic, Jock realised how good Ronnie was and put the needs of the team before his personal feelings.

Whatever Jock Stein's reasons, Celtic's gain was undoubtedly Hibs' loss since Ronnie was a tremendous goalkeeper. Ronnie Simpson was a nice man and an intelligent player. He had really good reflexes, could move quickly and had honed his goalkeeping technique through many years of experience.

Ronnie's successor, Willie Wilson, was just a young player starting out on his career. Willie came from Wallyford and had bags of ability. He was a likeable big guy and was really popular with everyone at Easter Road. Funnily enough one of my earliest memories of Willie playing for Hibs was a match against St Mirren when he got injured and ended up playing outfield. Willie cut his head and wasn't able to carry on in goal. He went off for treatment and came back on with his head wrapped in bandages. These were the days before substitutes were allowed so Peter Cormack had to go in goal. Peter performed like a natural and didn't let a goal in. Willie took up a position on the right wing. His bandage was sparkling white but his legs were even whiter. It must have been his Wallyford sun tan! Anyway, Willie was brilliant on the wing. He caused St Mirren lots of problems and the crowd cheered his every touch. We ended up winning 2–0.

Willie sometimes carried a few extra pounds but it wasn't through any lack of dedication. He trained really hard when it came to practising the art of goalkeeping. Fitness work was a wee bit different. During pre-season training, our physio Tom McNiven used to take us running up Arthur's Seat. Willie didn't like that at all. One year Tom told us to start running and not to stop until we reached the top. We all set off except Willie who stood motionless at the bottom. Tom shouted at the big goalie, 'Come on Willie, you as well, get yourself up there.'

Willie replied, 'No chance, there's no way I'm running up there.'

'Give me one good reason why you shouldn't run up there like the rest of the lads,' responded Tom.

Willie had the last word. 'Because I'm a specialist,' he said, 'and specialists dinnae run up hills.'

Willie made one of the best saves I have ever seen when we played Leeds United at Elland Road in the Fairs Cup. This was Don Revie's all conquering team but we were more than a match for them. Close to full time, they were awarded a free kick on the edge of our penalty area. Peter Lorimer, who had the hardest shot in football at that time, took it and sent a thunderbolt rocketing towards the top right-hand corner.

Willie dived full length and palmed the ball out. It was an amazing save. Unfortunately, the ball went straight back to Lorimer and he crashed it back towards the other side of Wilson's goal. Showing remarkable reflexes and agility for a big man, Willie flew back across his goal and pushed away this second attempt as well. Willie had just started wearing an all black goalkeeping strip at this time and had taken a bit of stick for it. Not this time. As our keeper got back to his feet after his tremendous double save, Jimmy O'Rourke turned to me and said, 'The Wallyford Bull has turned into the Black Panther.' Willie passed away some time ago and he is greatly missed by all his old team mates who had a lot of time for a friendly big fellow who was a very underrated goalkeeper.

Another Hibs keeper who was underrated was Thomson Allan. Thomson took over from Willie in the Hibs team and did well enough to eventually win a cap for Scotland. He was a quiet, unassuming lad off the field and he played the game in the same understated way. Thomson used to like to play left back in training and he wasn't at all bad. His kick outs from goal in matches were excellent and usually found a colleague a bit like Pepe Reina does with Liverpool today.

When Eddie Turnbull became manager of Hibs, one of the first things he did was to sign a goalkeeper. The man Eddie went for was Jim Herriot. Jim had been an excellent keeper for Dunfermline before moving to Birmingham City. He had moved on to South Africa before Eddie brought him home. It was a really good signing for us. As I said at the start of this chapter, every team needs a top goalie. In our Turnbull's Tornadoes team, Jim was that man. We all trusted him and we had every reason to do so. We called him 'Big Bob' because he had droopy eyelids like Robert Mitchum. He used to put dirt under his eyes to protect him against the glare of the sun or the floodlights. In one game when he made a couple of mistakes, he put more dirt under his eyes. Jimmy O'Rourke turned to me and said, 'Is he putting that stuff under his eyes or is he putting it in them?'

Jim didn't have many bad games though. He was quietly competitive and one of the best. Sadly, most folk remember Jim for the second leg of the European Cup Winners' Cup quarter final with Hajduk Split in 1973. We had won 4–2 at Easter Road and, in truth, it should have been a lot more. The return match was a difficult game played in front of a partisan crowd in a tightly packed ground. Jim didn't have his best game and we lost 3–0 and went out of a competition that we were good enough to win. We were all disappointed that night but no one more so than Jim. Eddie Turnbull must have been really down but to his credit he didn't rip into Jim after the game. He did move him on at the end of the season though, which was a shame because Jim still had a lot to offer. I would prefer to remember Jim for a game at Ibrox where we beat Rangers 1–0. Jim was magnificent that night. I'll never forget a couple of tremendous saves he pulled off from Derek Johnstone.

Eddie replaced Jim Herriot with another Jim. Jim McArthur came from Cowdenbeath and he was a good goalkeeper. When he performed to his best, he was absolutely outstanding. He wasn't consistent though. Jim was a bubbly character who didn't take life too seriously and enjoyed himself off the field. He was bright though and he used to combine PE teaching with his football. Jim gave Hibs great service over quite a few years. He was still there in fact when I came back as manager in 1982. I remember one game he played for me at Ibrox. He got a really bad gash in his ankle and we tried to get him to come off. Jim wouldn't hear of it and carried on although he was obviously suffering. We lost the game in the end but Jim was terrific, not only making some tremendous saves but also displaying real courage.

Eddie Turnbull then signed Mike McDonald to compete with Jim for the number one spot. Mike was a gentle giant. He was quiet both on and off the field and one of the nicest men you could meet. He had a lot of talent as a goalkeeper but never really made the most of that talent.

When I took over from Bertie Auld as manager in September 1982, we were not a great team. To be honest, I thought that we were in real danger of being relegated. Then I made my best ever signing. I asked Kenny Waugh, who was Hibs chairman at that time, to find the money to let me buy Alan Rough – and to his credit he did. When Brian Clough signed Peter Shilton for Nottingham Forest, a lot of people said that he had paid far too much for the big keeper. Clough had no doubts that the signing was a masterstroke. He declared that Shilton would save the team sixteen points per season and help them to win the league. He was right because that is exactly what happened. Alan Rough did the same for us. He helped us to win and draw games in the 1982–83 season that we would have lost without his consistently outstanding goal-keeping. He was the main reason that we stayed up.

Alan was a laid-back big lad but don't let that deceive you. He was a real professional. He gave everything in training and hated to lose a goal or a game. He really was top class and the rest of the lads looked up to him. I would go as far as to say that they found Roughie inspirational.

He was a real character as well. We used to organise an annual Christmas party for the players' children in the Fifties Club at the time Alan played for us. One of the players usually dressed up as Santa Claus. The man in question one year had a serious gambling problem and spent most of his spare time in the betting shop losing his money. He was never slow to borrow from his team mates in an attempt to recoup his losses either. However, he did agree to be Santa and to be fair to him, he was carrying out his duties really well. Then it was the turn of Roughie's children to go up and see Santa. The man in red sat them down next to him and said, 'And what would you like from Santa?' A loud shout came from the back of the room, 'They want their faither's money back for a start.' It was Alan Rough, of course, at his fun filled best.

Alan knew when to be serious though. I remember one game against Morton at Cappielow. It was really wet and we desperately needed to win. Surface water was forming on the pitch and it was proving difficult to judge the roll or the bounce of the ball. Alan spent the half time interval out on the field, getting our substitutes to roll the ball across the goalmouth he would be occupying in the second half to enable him to predict how the ball would behave. He gave an impeccable display after the break and we took a vital three points when Bobby Thomson scored, giving us a 1–0 victory.

A lot of players are extrovert and noisy. Before a game they will be loud in the changing room. After a defeat, they will throw things around and make a fuss. Roughie was never like that. He was always quiet but don't let that fool anyone that he didn't care. He cared all right but he let his goal-keeping do his talking for him. His calm confidence and obvious ability transformed our team's self-belief in the dressing room and on the pitch. Alan's influence at Hibs was massive.

He had some great games for us but probably had his best spell when John Blackley took the team to the 1985 League Cup Final. He played fantastically well against both Rangers and Celtic in that competition. He saved penalties in both games and was largely responsible for us reaching the final. When we got there, of course, we met Alex Ferguson's Aberdeen and they were just too good for us.

Alan was happy at Hibs with John and me but he seemed less settled when Alex Miller took over. Miller obviously thought that Alan's best days were behind him because he signed Andy Goram from Oldham. Alan actually moved on to Celtic next so he clearly still had something to offer.

Andy Goram was another great Hibs goalie. He wasn't the biggest but he was an amazing athlete. I remember one game not long after Goram had come to Easter Road. I was sitting in the stand with George Stewart watching the match and one of the opposition players let fly with a rocket shot. George and I said 'goal' at the same time but we were both wrong. Goram flew across his goal and palmed the ball to safety. It was a save to take your breath away. Andy made plenty of saves of that type for Hibs and was definitely one of our best ever keepers.

I always found him to be a really pleasant, friendly man when I met him but his cheery nature hid a fiercely competitive streak that was evident in his total love of all sports. Goram was a complete natural, of course. He played cricket for Scotland and was a top class snooker player too. He liked to enjoy himself off the field but when it came to training or a match he gave his all.

His all round talents were such that he could easily have been an outfield player. He even managed to score two goals for Hibs. One was against Morton when a kick out carried the whole length of the field and bounced over their goalkeeper. The other was in a League Cup match with Clydebank at Easter Road. The game went to penalties and Hibs had to score their last one to win and go through to the next round. To everyone's amazement, Andy Goram came forward to take it. He was so confident of scoring that he didn't even bother to take off his goalkeeping gloves. He strolled up and slotted the ball home in style. He then motioned to the rest of the team to follow him over to the fans to celebrate.

Andy was very fond of the late Kenny McLean. I think he saw Kenny as a sort of father figure to him. Kenny is probably best remembered for leading the successful Hands Off Hibs campaign in 1990 to keep our club out of the clutches of Wallace Mercer but he was also a great support to me when I was manager. He was vice chairman of Hibs at that time and would urge me to go out and sign any player I fancied. When I asked him how we could afford this or that player, his reply was always the same. Kenny would say, 'Don't worry about the money. We'll sort that out later.' Probably wisely, his fellow directors used to inject a bit of caution and we would end up staying within our budget. Kenny was a great man though, and he and Andy Goram got on like a house on fire.

After we sold Andy to Rangers for £1 million in 1991 he went on to become Scotland's regular first choice goalkeeper. In my opinion, he was no better during his time at Ibrox than he had been at Easter Road, yet his caps while he was at Hibs were few and far between.

When Alex Miller signed John Burridge to replace Goram, a few eyebrows were raised. Budgie was close to forty and, in a lot of people's opinion, he was past his sell by date. He wasn't though. He was still a sound keeper and a great organiser. He was some character as well. People say that the school of goalkeepers is full of eccentrics. If that's the case, then Budgie was an Oxford graduate. He may have been a wee bit off the wall but there was a purpose to his eccentricity. One of his favourite routines was to place a stack of oranges next to his wife on the couch when they were watching television in the evening. Budgie would sit on the opposite sofa and every so often, without any warning, his wife would throw one of the oranges at him. He would always back himself to catch it. Now this is probably not how your average couple spends a quiet night in but I'm sure it helped to keep Budgie's reflexes nice and sharp.

Budgie was brilliant when Hibs won the League Cup in 1991. His save from Ally McCoist in the semi final was one of the very best and crucial to our eventual success. He was lying on his line when a shot rebounded from the post straight to McCoist. How he got up in time to dive through the air and clutch McCoist's follow-up shot I'll never know, but he did and it helped to take us to the final.

At that time, the great goalies just seemed to keep on coming at Easter Road. When Budgie moved on, Alex Miller brought in Jim Leighton. I was Assistant Manager to Alex Ferguson at Aberdeen when Jim first broke through. It was a measure of his quality that someone as good as Bobby Clark had to make way for him. He was an absolutely top quality goalkeeper and, in no time at all, he and his defensive partners Alex McLeish and Willie Miller had established themselves in the Scottish international team.

One thing I did notice about Jim during my time at Pittodrie was that he had a serious and sensitive side to him. If he made a mistake, which wasn't very often, or if his form had dipped slightly, Jim would take it to heart and get a bit down on himself. We saw this when he moved to Manchester United.

Alex Ferguson had signed Jim not long after moving from Aberdeen to Old Trafford, believing he could be United's first choice keeper for years to come. Jim's first season had been reasonable but he hadn't played consistently to his Aberdeen form. When United met Crystal Palace in the FA Cup Final, Jim didn't have his best game and the match ended 3–3. Alex decided to leave Jim out for the replay and brought in Les Sealey to replace him. United won 1–0 and Jim was devastated.

He was really upset by his manager's actions and you could argue that Alex's decision was harsh. Equally, you could say that Fergie was vindicated as United won the match and the cup.

Managers have to take tough decisions and Alex Ferguson took one that day. That it greatly upset Jim Leighton there is no doubt. His confidence and self-belief took a massive knock and his career went backwards. He was at Dundee when Alex Miller decided to go for him and it proved to be an inspired move. Jim slowly but surely rebuilt his reputation and proved to be a magnificent goalkeeper for Hibs. He was totally safe and reliable but also capable of producing the miracle save. His one weakness was his kicking. He wasn't comfortable with the ball at his feet and this caused him problems in a few games. I can remember a derby game at Easter Road when Jim got caught in possession and this led to Hearts scoring.

When it came to handling the ball though, Jim was top class. If Alan Rough was my best signing as Hibs manager, then Jim Leighton came close to being Alex Miller's best capture during his time with us. As somebody who had worked with Jim at the start of his career, it was great to see his confidence return and to see him regain his place in the Scotland team. Like a lot of Hibs fans, I was sorry to see him go when he chose to return to Pittodrie in 1997 and to be honest, Hibs haven't had a settled goalkeeper since.

From the time Jim moved on, we have had a succession of keepers. Some of them have showed brief promise but haven't sustained it. Others have just not been good enough and have cost us games and points. Jim Duffy bought Olly Gottskalksson to replace Jim Leighton and he paid quite a bit of money for him. I think it's fair to say that it was a move that never really worked out. 'Olly the Goalie' had his moments. He was great in the last game of the 1997–98 season when we beat Falkirk at Easter Road on the day we received the First Division Championship. Olly saved a Scott Crabbe penalty that day and looked a world beater. He wasn't reliable though, and it wasn't long before Duffy replaced him with Chris Reid.

Chris had been at Hibs for a while but he was still a young goalkeeper. I liked Chris as a goalie and I thought that he had a good chance of making it with Hibs. But it didn't work out for him, and one of Alex McLeish's first moves when he took over from Duffy was to bring in Bryan Gunn from Norwich.

Big Bryan was another goalie I worked with at Aberdeen. He used to keep in his boss's good books by doing a bit of babysitting for Fergie. It didn't do him any good though because he had to move to England to get regular first team football. He had matured nicely as a keeper by the time he came to Easter Road. He started really well but got an injury that finished his career quite early in his time with Hibs. Bryan went home to Norwich and recently was made their manager. Sadly, he wasn't a success as they sacked him only two games into the 2009–10 season. Most managers lose their job sooner or later. Bryan's sacking was very much in the sooner category.

After Gunn was injured, McLeish brought in Nick Colgan. The fact that Colgan had never managed a competitive first team start for Chelsea should have told us something. He wasn't the worst goalkeeper in the world but he was a long way from being the best. McLeish then tried Tony Caig but he was no better.

When Bobby Williamson took up the reins at Easter Road, he wasted no time in signing the Swedish goalkeeper Daniel Andersson. I thought that Andersson was a really good keeper. He was brilliant against Rangers in the 2004 League Cup semi final. He saved a penalty during the game itself and then another two during the penalty shootout. I was surprised and a wee bit disappointed when he was allowed to leave at the end of that season.

It seems like every new Hibs manager in recent years has made it his first priority to sign a new goalkeeper. Tony Mowbray was no exception. Tony signed Simon Brown from Colchester. Now big Mowbray made same great signings for the Hibs but Simon Brown wasn't one of them. I remember him standing, watching a header roll into the net against Hearts at Tynecastle. Every Hibs fan behind Brown's goal knew that the ball was going in but Simon obviously thought that it was going past. Needless to say, the ball ended up in the net and our goalkeeper ended up looking extremely embarrassed.

Brown's worst howler was against Rangers at Easter Road. As Charlie Adam lined up a free kick, the keeper got his positioning all wrong and left a huge gap at his near post. Everybody except Brown knew what was going to happen next. Adam curled the ball into the inviting gap that our goalkeeper had left for him. Brown held his head in his hands. It's a wonder he didn't drop it.

After one season of Simon Brown, Tony Mowbray decided he needed a change between the posts and brought in Zbigniew Malkowski. The big Pole looked the part but he was another accident waiting to happen. At times he seemed good, but just when you thought that he had cut out his habit of making costly errors, he would come up with another one. He didn't help himself by choosing games against Hearts for his worst performances. Most Hibs fans will forgive their players for the occasional error, but when a player keeps making mistakes in derby games his popularity rating is guaranteed to plummet. Probably Malkowski's worst game was the Scottish Cup semi final against Hearts in 2006. He replicated Brown's bloomer against Rangers by giving Paul Hartley the opportunity to beat him at his front post with a free kick. He wasn't too clever for the next goal either and Hearts eventually beat us 4–0, which was a real sore one.

Malkowski was never going to last. Mowbray replaced him with young Andy McNeil who, despite being capable of the occasional superb save, was too small and inconsistent. When Mowbray left for West Brom, John Collins took his place. It was no surprise to anybody when John said that he was looking for a goalkeeper. His choice was Yves Makalambay. Big Yves has the height and the agility and should be a top keeper but he's not. He's too casual, lacks concentration and lets in too many avoidable goals. Mind you, he can make great saves. It's no good though if you follow a top stop by throwing one in, and Yves chucks in more than his fair share. Every time he shows signs of improvement, he lapses into his previous bad ways. The two second-half goals he conceded against Rangers at Christmas 2009 are a case in point.

Mixu Paatelainen talked a lot about signing a new goal-keeper when he replaced John Collins but he never quite got round to it on a permanent basis. Mixu did bring in Gregorz Szamoltulski on loan but he didn't look like the permanent answer to our goalkeeping problem either. When Mixu surprised everyone by resigning in the summer of 2009, John Hughes returned to Easter Road as manager. John had plenty to say in his early days in his post and the most predictable of his comments was when he announced that he was looking for a new goalkeeper. He didn't take long to find one and brought in the former Arsenal keeper Graham Stack. Stack started well before being sidelined with a back injury. John then brought in the former Motherwell keeper Graeme Smith who also impressed in his early games. Mark Brown came from Celtic to further augment what Yogi calls his 'goalkeeping school' in the 2010 January transfer window. Whether Stack, Brown or Smith will provide a long-term solution to the challenge of finding an established goalkeeper, only time will tell. It would certainly be nice to have a reliable number one again.

That's in the future though and as I select my goalkeeper for my dream team, I am looking back. Goalkeeper may have been a recent problem for Hibs but that certainly wasn't the case in the past. As this chapter shows we have been blessed with some magnificent last lines of defence and I have found it really hard to choose just one of them for my team. After a lot of thought, I've drawn up a short list of three. With apologies to great keepers like Tommy Younger, Ronnie Simpson and Jim Herriot, I've narrowed my choice down to Alan Rough, Andy Goram and Jim Leighton.

It wasn't easy to leave out so many top class keepers. It's even harder to pick one from my final three. Rough, Goram and Leighton were all great shot stoppers. A quality keeper should save everything that is saveable. My three definitely did that. The very best though can make what I call 'miracle saves'. That is to say, they can keep out shots that they had no right to get close to. Again, Roughie, Andy and Jim were capable of that. They could all take your breath away with a spectacular save when you had resigned yourself to the ball ending up in the Hibs net. They could also all come and gather the high ball. They knew when to stay on their line and when to leave it. A lot of goalkeepers find that a hard judgement to make. Rough, Goram and Leighton made the decision instinctively and usually made it correctly too. All three of my keepers were brave. They thought nothing of risking injury by throwing themselves at the feet of an onrushing striker or diving through a maze of bodies to get the ball.

I can only separate them on two counts. The first is temperament. Jim could be hard on himself because he was such a perfectionist. If Roughie or Goram made a mistake, they would quickly dismiss it from their mind. Jim would dwell on it because that was his nature. If you were playing in the San Siro or the Nou Camp, Jim would probably get a little bit uptight. Alan and Andy would relish the challenge. The bigger the occasion, the more they liked it.

Rough and Goram were also comfortable with the ball at their feet. They could control it under pressure and make a good clearance. They weren't averse to the odd foray outside their area. They would anticipate danger and almost act as a sweeper by coming out of their box to collect a through ball and snuff out a promising move. Leighton wasn't so strong in this area and sometimes got himself into a bit of a fankle when it came to controlling or clearing a ball with his feet.

Reluctantly then, I've had to eliminate Jim. The fact that I'm leaving out such a top notch goalie is a compliment to my final two. How do I choose between Rough and Goram then? The answer is with the greatest of difficulty. In the end, I have gone for Alan Rough for one reason and one reason only. Andy Goram was good at Oldham and Hibs but he wasn't fully recognised for the goalkeeper he was until he signed for Rangers. Roughie on the other hand was a Scotland regular while playing for Partick Thistle. He also shone in a struggling Hibs team. It is easy to be successful in a trophy-winning team but difficult to do so in a team in adversity. Despite spending most of his club career with teams that were fighting for survival, Alan Rough still stood out as a goal-keeper of the highest class and that is why I have chosen him for my Hibernian Dream Team. I suppose if I'm being totally honest, I've also got a soft spot for Roughie because he kept my Hibs team in the top division. When I signed him, I knew that I had got a good one. I didn't realise quite how good till I saw him in training every day and in matches every week. Goram, Rough and Leighton sound like a firm of solicitors but for me big Alan is the senior partner.

2

FABULOUS FULL BACKS

When a football team runs out for a match these days, you could never tell a player's position just by looking at his build. They are all athletes now and all have similar body shapes. It wasn't like that when I first joined Hibs in the early sixties. Wingers were wee and nippy, centre halves were big and burly and full backs were small and stocky.

Joe McLelland was Hibs' left back when I started my career at Easter Road and he was very much of the old school. Barrel chested and bulky, Joe was every inch the old-fashioned full back. He was a defender pure and simple and never bothered with luxuries like overlapping. Joe was a nice man – unless you were playing against him. If a winger found himself one on one with Joe, he might get by him but he wouldn't go very far. Joe was a real hard tackler and if you went past him you usually came down not long afterwards. There were a lot of full backs in that mould back then. Tommy Banks of Bolton and Bobby Shearer of Rangers are two others who spring to mind.

As I said, Joe wasn't one to venture forward too often but he did get his name on the score sheet once that I remember. When Hibs beat Airdrie 11–1 at Broomfield in 1959, Joe managed a collector's piece of a goal. He almost scored a priceless goal in the 1958 Scottish Cup Final against Clyde.

As Hibs chased an equaliser, Joe made a rare foray forward. He hit a shot like a rocket that looked like it was heading for the roof of the net. Unfortunately, Clyde's Mike Clinton got in the way of the ball. He was knocked unconscious and the ball rebounded to safety. Hibs' hopes of lifting the cup disappeared with it.

Joe's full back partner was John Grant. We called John 'The Duke' because he was always immaculately dressed. He was ahead of his time as a full back. He had terrific pace and was a really good user of the ball. He was quite happy to come forward. He was chosen for Scotland in the late fifties and made his debut in a match against Wales. Matt Busby was Scotland's manager that day and Denis Law was playing his first game as well. Scotland won 3–0, Denis scored and John Grant played really well.

In Hibs' famous 4–3 Scottish Cup win over Hearts in 1958, Hugh Shaw pushed John forward to inside right and he put in an excellent performance. He was just a good all-round footballer. He was helpful to the young players too. He always had a word of encouragement for us and he supported me a lot when I was starting out. Ronnie Simpson, who played with the very best, rated Grant really highly.

John Fraser took over from Grant. John had started as a centre forward, had a go as a winger and then found his best position at right back. He was good in the air and safe on the ground. He had a sound football brain and always kept his cool. I think he played his best football for Hibs under Jock Stein. One of his greatest games though was the 3–2 victory over Barcelona in 1961. As Barcelona pressed for an equaliser towards the end, John organised the defence, kept everyone calm and saw us through to a famous win.

John used to give me a lift to training. He did some work with his farmer father-in-law Danny Hanlon and he had a pink, hand-painted van. There were buckets of pigswill in the back of the van but I would sit in the front with John. However, some days John would pick up his mother en route. When that happened, I had to go in the back and I can tell you it wasn't the best. When I look back now, I often think to myself, 'I wonder if Franco Baresi ever went to training in the back of a van full of pigswill?'

When John retired, he became a coach at Hibs and he was a good one. He was always pleasant but nobody mucked him around. When he spoke, we listened because he always had something useful to say. He was always telling us not to try to kick the ball too hard. He would tell us, 'Just guide it and time it. That's all you need to do.' John was a handsome man and he's still looking good in his seventies. He must have Cliff Richard's secret of eternal youth because he looks nothing like his age.

Walter Galbraith signed John Parke from Linfield to partner John Fraser at full back. He had seen Parke playing well for Northern Ireland in a home international match against Scotland and had brought him to Hibs. It was a great signing because Parkey was top class. He was cultured, constructive and sound in defence. His hair was always perfectly quiffed and Brylcreemed and he looked like a young Robert De Niro playing the part of a gigolo.

As an experienced international, he took it upon himself to help develop us young players. After a win, I would be coming off feeling pleased with myself when Parkey would come across and say quietly, 'That won't do, you know.' At training on Monday, he would tell you exactly what hadn't been good enough. It was always sound advice and taking it on board made me a better player.

John was a big pal of Willie Hamilton. You could say that they were fellow travellers. They had some legendary sessions.

One of their most famous was when Parkey was in hospital recovering from an operation. Willie went to visit him and brought supplies. This was a 'cairry-in' rather than a 'cairry-oot'. John had a ward to himself and when Willie arrived, he shut the door and the two pals got down to business. It didn't take them long to finish the stock of refreshments that Willie had supplied. They then decided that it was time for a sing song. When the nurse came to check on Parke, she found Willie and him with their arms round each other singing their hearts out. I never did find out what happened next.

John Parke did like to enjoy himself. He kept up the Irish tradition of being exceptionally skilled in the art of relaxation. Unlike his friend Hamilton though, he knew when to stop and he trained hard. It was no surprise when Sunderland signed Parkey. They paid £40,000 for him, which gave Hibs a good profit on their original investment. That was a lot of money in those days but Parke was worth every penny. He was right out of the top drawer.

His replacement wasn't bad either. Jock Stein was manager when Sunderland came in for Parke. He refused to sanction the deal until he had signed Joe Davis from Third Lanark for £7000. When Davis was safely secured, the Parke deal went ahead. Joe was a great servant to Hibs. He played to his strengths and kept it simple and was amazingly consistent. He once went four seasons in a row without missing a league game, which says something for his fitness. He was a great penalty taker too.

He scored thirty-one goals for Hibs and they were nearly all penalties. He only missed a couple but they were vital. He missed one at Tynecastle that cost us a Scottish Cup tie against Hearts and he missed against Hamburg in the Fairs Cup when we went out on away goals. Joe was a cheery character and didn't let defeats get him down. If we lost, you would never have known it from Joe's post-match demeanour. That used to really annoy some of the lads who thought that he didn't care. He cared all right. He just believed that when a game had gone there was no point on brooding over it. Joe preferred to look forward positively to the next game.

Somebody else who didn't get too down after a defeat was Frank Haffey, the Celtic goalkeeper. Big Frank was in goal when Scotland lost 9–3 to England at Wembley. In the showers after the game, Denis Law was suicidal. He couldn't believe it when he heard the sound of singing from the bath next door. He went to see who the singer was and, to his amazement, it was the man who had just let in nine goals. I think it's fair to say that Denis was not impressed with his goalkeeper's behaviour. It's probably best not to repeat here what he said to Haffey but I am sure that you could have a good guess at the gist of Denis' comments.

Bobby Duncan partnered Joe Davis at right back. I liked Bobby as a man and as a player. Although the media praised Tommy Gemmell of Celtic for being Scotland's first top class attacking full back, take it from me that Bobby Duncan was going forward long before Gemmell and doing it well too. Bobby knew when to overlap and when to stay back. He judged his moment and timed his runs perfectly.

Bobby never joined the attack with more effect than against Napoli in 1967. They had beaten us 4–1 in Naples and came to Easter Road for the return leg full of confidence. They were actually overconfident and it was to cost them dearly. In the first couple of minutes of the game, Bobby came forward up the slope. The Italian defenders backed off and he hit a thunderbolt with his left foot. The ball sailed into the roof of Dino Zoff's net. I reckon Bobby was about thirty yards out when he hit his shot. Mind you every time I discuss this goal with somebody these days, the distance of Bobby's strike seems to get bigger. Like the fish that got away, Bobby's goal grows in the telling. It was a great goal though, and the manner of it and the fact that it came so early in the game set the crowd alight and rocked the Italians. They never recovered and we won 5–0 with the other goals coming from Pat Quinn, Peter Cormack, Colin Stein and myself. Funnily enough, that was Bobby Duncan's only first team goal for Hibs.

Like a lot of full backs, Bobby started off as a forward but found his true niche further back. He was on top of his game when he broke his leg in a match against Celtic at Easter Road in 1968 after being tackled by big John Hughes. Bobby was never the same after that, which was a shame because there had been talk about top English clubs being poised to bid for him before the injury.

I remember when we took part in a tournament in North America in the sixties. We were treated like kings and spent seven weeks in five-star hotels. We were all getting a wee bit homesick by this time and before our last qualifying match we had a team meeting. We were playing Glentoran and if we won, we would move on to Los Angeles for the next stage of the competition. When our manager Bob Shankly asked us what we thought, a few of us made it clear that we were ready for home. We said that we would try to win the match but that we weren't going to kill ourselves. Bobby perked up: 'I need to get hame. I've got a week at Butlin's in Filey booked up with my mates and I cannae miss that.'

In the event, the game finished in a draw and we were on our way. We had been pampered and had sampled the best of everything for weeks on end but Bobby just couldn't wait to join his pals at Butlin's. It just shows that you can get too much of a good thing.

When Bobby got injured, Chris Shevlane came in. Chris was small, stocky and red haired. He had played for Hearts and had also had a spell with Celtic. By the time he came to Hibs, Chris was probably past his peak but he still had something to offer. He was rock solid in defence and not afraid to come forward. He did not lack confidence and had a habit of referring to himself in the third person. He called himself 'The Shev' and would say things like, 'What was the Shev like today? Have you ever seen anything as good as that?' Another time, after a game as we sat in the dressing room, he piped up out of the blue, 'The Shev's definitely too good for this place.' He wasn't but he was a more than decent full back.

By the time Shev was moving on, a young centre half called John Brownlie had joined up from Edina Hibs. We were playing St Johnstone at Perth and John came on as a sub at right back in what was then an unfamiliar position for him. He was a revelation. We were all looking at each other and saying, 'We've found a player here.'

He was a great tackler, really comfortable on the ball and totally at home in the other team's penalty area. Most defenders get the proverbial nosebleed when they find themselves deep in opposition territory. That was never the case with John. He would hit the goal line and whip over a great cross or he would go through and have a shot himself. He began to make and score goals regularly, carving out a reputation for himself in the process.

By the time he was nineteen, he had been capped by Scotland. He made his debut in Moscow against Russia and I had the honour of being Scotland captain that night. When Eddie Turnbull took over as manager, he signed Alex Edwards and John. Alex and I formed a triangle on the right side of field in Eddie's great Tornadoes team. It was a real pleasure to play with John and Alex. They were such top-notch players that they made it really easy for me.

John was outstanding when we won the League Cup in

1972. He scored two goals against Airdrie in the quarter final and followed that up by scoring the winner against Rangers in the semi. When it came to the final, Jock Stein paid John the ultimate compliment. He switched Jimmy Johnstone to the left wing in the hope of curbing John's attacking runs. It didn't stop John from having a great game and he was terrific again a few weeks later when we beats Hearts 7–0 at Tynecastle on New Year's Day 1973.

Sadly in our next game against East Fife, John sustained a bad leg break after a tackle by Ian Printy. John always stressed that it was a complete accident and that Printy was totally blameless. He was out for nearly a year and when he came back that special something that had made him so incredible was missing. He was still a top player but that wee bit extra just wasn't there any more.

John was a bit of a character off the field. One night, George Stewart, John and I were sitting in our hotel room. We were in Dublin to play Bohemians. All of a sudden, John said, 'I've been here before you know.'

'In this hotel?' asked George.

'No,' said John. 'I've been here before.'

George tried again. 'Do you mean in Ireland?'

'No,' said Brownlie. 'I've been in this world before and I can even remember who I was.'

'Who were you?' I asked.

'I was Davy Crockett in my last life,' said John with a totally straight face.

We hadn't been drinking and as far as we could tell John was completely serious. I turned to George and said, 'Well fancy that. The best right back in Scotland is the king of the wild frontier.'

On a football pitch though, John was peerless. He would receive the ball from Jim Herriot on the edge of our box, wait till the oncoming forward made a tackle and then pull the ball back with the sole of his boot. The forward would go sliding past and John would move imperiously forward with the ball. Alex Edwards used to worry that John would lose the ball and say to him, 'I wish you wouldnae dae that.' John kept on doing it though, and he kept on coming away with the ball.

We had signed Des Bremner from Deveronvale to understudy John and young Des must have been resigned to a long spell waiting in the wings. All of a sudden, with John's injury he got his chance. Replacing John was never going to be easy but Des approached it in the right way. He played to his strengths and kept it simple and soon won over the fans. Des was a really nice lad with a lilting Highland accent and because he played in a much less flamboyant way than the great Brownlie had done, people underestimated his ability. He became a midfield player, of course, and won caps. He also got a big money move to Aston Villa and won a European Cup winners' medal with them. You don't achieve these things without being a top player and Des was exactly that. He is in a select band with his European Cup winners' medal. The only other players to have played for Hibs and won the European Cup are Ronnie Simpson, Bertie Auld, George Best and Franck Sauzée. The last I heard of Des he was still down south and working for the PFA.

John's Brownlie's partner in Turnbull's Tornadoes was, of course, Erich Schaedler. Willie MacFarlane was the manager who signed Erich from Stirling Albion. Willie was never a man for an understatement and when he signed Erich he gave him a massive build up. He told us after training one day, 'I've just signed a left back from Stirling Albion and he's a cross between Facchetti of Inter Milan and Tommy Gemmell.' In truth, Erich wasn't quite that good but he was still a really superb player.

He could run like the wind and he had a tackle like a sledgehammer. One of his first games for Hibs was a friendly against the Polish team Gornik. Peter Cormack got in the way of one of Erich's crunching tackles and ended up going off on a stretcher. I could see the Polish players looking at each other as if to say, 'If that's what he does to his own team, what will he do to us?'

Erich had a bit of style about him. He had this really classy convertible sports car. I lived close to where he stayed in Rosewell and he used to give me a lift to training. Even on the coldest, frostiest winter's day, he would have the roof down. One day it was so cold that a polar bear would have needed an overcoat but, as usual, Erich had the car's roof down. He was wearing a sweater and a pair of designer sunglasses. I was well wrapped up but still feeling the cold. Erich grinned and said, 'This is cool.' It wasn't cool – it was freezing.

That car was Erich's pride and joy. One day he left it at the ground and we jogged down to Hawkhill for training. Training had just started when the heavens opened. It was like a monsoon. Of course, Erich had left his car parked with the roof down. You could see that he wanted to ask Eddie Turnbull if he could run back to the ground and put his roof up but he was too scared. By the time we got back, Erich's lovely car was in a sorry state. His face was an absolute picture.

Erich's most spectacular goal for Hibs came against Partick Thistle in the Scottish Cup in 1972. He took one of his famous long throws from the touchline opposite Thistle's corner flag. The ball was headed back to him and he absolutely belted it on the volley towards Alan Rough in the Partick goal. It could have gone anywhere but flashed past Roughie and ended up in the net. It was the kind of goal that Popeye would have scored. Erich's dad was German, of course, so it was fitting that when he was picked for Scotland the match was against Germany.

I couldn't believe it when Erich committed suicide. It was round about Christmas time. I had received a phone call from Leith CID to ask if I knew where Erich was. Apparently his dogs were at home on their own and no one knew where Erich had gone. Tragically he had gone to a forest in the Borders and taken his own life. To this day I have no idea why he would do that.

In the eighties, Alan Sneddon was usually right back. Bertie Auld had signed Alan from Celtic and he helped to get Hibs promoted. Alan had played enough games for Celtic before he moved to Hibs to qualify for a League winners' medal with them so he picked up a Premier League medal and a First Division medal in the same season. Alan played for me when I was manager and he was a big, honest, wholehearted player who never hid in games. These were difficult times for Hibs and some players were content to keep a low profile and take the easy option.

Alan was always prepared to try something and even though it didn't always come off, he was the kind of player managers like – brave and committed. Alan stayed long enough with Hibs to earn a testimonial. We beat Aston Villa and Keith Wright scored all four Hibs goals. Kenny Dalglish guested for Hibs that night and his reward for doing that was a black pudding supper and a bottle of Cream Soda. He had missed these delicacies during his time in England. The media portray Kenny as dour but he isn't. When I played with him with Scotland, he was always a good laugh. He liked to tell jokes and the Christmas cracker variety were his favourites.

I also used Ally Brazil at right back when I was in charge at Easter Road. Ally was a versatile player when he was at Hibs. He played at full back, in central defence and in midfield for the club. He had his limitations and he wasn't the most elegant of players but what he did give you was total commitment. I knew that if I picked Ally, he would give me everything for every minute of every game.

Ally used to get a hard time from the fans. A lot of players would have gone under from that kind of pressure but Ally never did. He kept his head up and he kept going. Alan Rough, on the other hand, was only used to success as a player. He regularly received the acclaim of the crowds and came to accept that as his right. Towards the end of his time at Easter Road, Alan went through a bad spell. One day he got some stick from the fans. This was unheard of and as it turned out, it was a one-off incident, but it shook Roughie up. I remember him telling me, 'It came as a real shock to me. I had never experienced it before and I didn't like it. It really made me admire somebody like Ally Brazil who was criticised by the supporters week in and week out but took it all in his stride and continued to give everything for the team.'

When Alex Miller became manager, Willie Miller was his regular right back. They don't come any harder than Willie. I used to think of him as the silent assassin. He was a great defender and a cast iron tackler. If Willie knocked you down, he would step on you as he went after the ball. He had a mean streak and that's what made him so good. No forward relished facing Willie and it wasn't hard to understand why. He could go forward but usually stayed back. I think he lacked the confidence in his attacking ability to go forward more often.

Willie Miller was one of the hardest players ever to play for Hibs but he had a soft side too. Alex Miller tells a story about Willie when he had a headache one Saturday before a match. The manager told him to take some paracetamol and he would be fine. In the dressing room at quarter to three,

Willie didn't look too great. Alex asked him how he was and he said that he still had a really sore head. Alex asked if he had taken the paracetamol as directed and Willie admitted that he hadn't.

'Why not?' demanded the manager.

'Because when my mother gives me paracetamol she always puts jam on the tablets,' replied the rock hard full back.

Willie's main full back partner was Graham Mitchell. Mitch was a great servant to Hibs. He could play in central defence and give the team a shift in midfield but he was happiest at left back. He was unassuming but full of enthusiasm. He was energetic as well. He did his defensive work quietly and well and he could get up and down the touchline when he wanted to.

When Alex McLeish took over, he signed a top left back in Ulrik Laursen. Ulrik was recommended to Alex and he went over to Denmark to watch him. Within ten minutes, Alex had seen enough. He could see that big Laursen was an athlete and a player. After furtively looking round to make sure no other scouts or managers were there, Alex left. He wasted no time in signing Ulrik the next day. The big fella did well for Hibs and I was sorry to see him sold to Celtic where he never really settled.

I have never understood why the Old Firm sign players and then don't play them. Rangers did this with Kenny Miller the first time around and did it again more recently with Alan Gow. Celtic did the same with Derek Riordan before his move back to Hibs and they have also done it with Chris Killen and Paddy McCourt.

I was a bit taken aback when Alex McLeish signed Ulises de La Cruz and paid £750,000 for him. Ulises was great going forward but he was poor defensively and he struck me as being lazy as well. He showed his potential when he played so brilliantly against AEK Athens but he wasn't consistent and I think we were lucky to make a profit on him when we sold him to Aston Villa.

Tony Mowbray had two cracking full backs during his time in charge at Easter Road. Steven Whittaker was a great, young, attacking right back. He occasionally lost concentration at the back but he has a lot of talent and I think that he can go on and have a great career. Steven has scored twice against Hibs since leaving us to join Rangers. He'll have to cut that out.

When Tony brought in David Murphy on a free transfer from Middlesbrough, he made a top signing. David was impressive right from the word go and he just got better and better. The thing that struck me about him was his first touch. You could fire a ball at him from any angle at any pace and he would drop it at his feet with one touch. He made it look easy as well. David was somebody else who was good going forward but he was really sound defensively as well. The one thing he lacked was a little bit of pace.

David's first goal for Hibs was against Celtic and his last goal for us was against the same team at Parkhead in December 2007. David never made a secret of the fact that he hoped to return to England one day but he always gave Hibs total respect. For a man who cost us nothing, he gave us three and a half years' great service and brought in a good fee when he left. I've a lot of time for David Murphy and I wish him well with his new club.

Since John Hughes has come in as manager, he has struggled to find the right full back combination. One player who might help him out is Ian Murray. Ian is a versatile player who can do a turn in a number of positions. He is a steady central defender and a decent left back. When he plays left back, he makes his tackles and is able to get forward effectively as well. Personally, I like Ian in midfield. I think that the team needs his drive and enthusiasm in that area.

The choice of right back for my dream team is easy. There is only one contender and that is the great John Brownlie. It was a privilege to play with John. I know he thinks that his skills didn't diminish after his leg break, but I am not so sure. Before his injury John was a truly great player. He was a right winger in a right back's jersey but he never neglected the defensive side of the game. When he came back from his injury, John was still good enough to win a few more Scotland caps. But if he hadn't sustained such a bad injury, he would have been Scotland's regular right back for ten years. At his best, John would have walked into any team in the world and he's just walked straight into mine.

My left back might surprise a few people. It was really hard to leave out a player as good as Erich Schaedler but that is what I've done. I've gone for John Parke. John didn't play a lot of games for Hibs. That was partly because he was so good that Sunderland wasted no time in snapping him up. He also had a couple of injuries during his time with us, which caused him to miss games. In fact, John only played twenty-one games for Hibs. I've still picked him though, and that shows you how highly I rate him. He was calm and authoritative and the complete full back.

Like all my dream team, he was most of all a very good all round footballer. Some players specialise in one area of the game. John, like all my selections, was skilled in every area of the game. He also kept Willie Hamilton in order for a couple of years so he definitely had something going for him.

Joking apart, a full back combination of the two Johns – Brownlie and Parke – would frighten the life out of any opposition. They would snuff out any attacking threat and cause havoc when they went forward. That's why I am delighted to have them in my team.

3

CLASSY, COMMANDING CENTRAL DEFENDERS

Nowadays we're used to thinking of centre halves forming partnerships of two. When Hibs won the League Cup in 1991, our central defenders were Tommy McIntyre and Gordon Hunter. When we won it again in 2007, Chris Hogg and Rob Jones were in the middle of the back four. When I first started out in football though, it was completely different. In the fifties and early sixties, teams employed a 2–3–5 formation. There were two full backs who were out and out defenders and a centre half who covered the central defensive area. The centre half was also a defender pure and simple. He would be flanked by two half backs and the other five outfield players were forwards. In truth, one of the half backs was usually more defensively minded than his partner and he would do his best to give the centre half a bit of support. In the main though, the centre half was on his own at the back.

The first two centre halves I remember at Hibs were John Paterson and Jackie Plenderleith. They were old-fashioned pivots, which was the name given to central defenders in those days, and played without a partner. They were similar players. John played in the great Famous Five team, of course, and Jackie was his successor. Both John and Jackie were steady, tidy players. They weren't flamboyant and they did their job with minimum fuss and maximum efficiency. Jackie left Hibs for Manchester City and was capped by Scotland during his time at Maine Road. John would probably have picked up Scotland caps if he hadn't been born in England.

Another centre half in my early days was big Duncan Falconer who came from Lochend. Duncan's nickname was 'The Ace' because he could play at the back or up front. He got quite a few goals in one season when he played mainly as a forward but I liked him as a defender. We got on well but I remember that he sorted me out verbally in one of my earliest games. Willie Wilson in goal had made a mistake and I bawled him out. Duncan said to Willie, 'If he ever talks to you like that again, kick his backside.' In fact, he may have used a different word than backside. Mind you, you could never be annoyed with Willie for long because he was such a nice big guy.

When Duncan left Hibs, he joined the police force in England. His senior officer contacted me recently because Duncan was retiring and they wanted a photograph of him playing for Hibs. When I told the policeman that I was happy to oblige for 'The Ace', he was surprised that Duncan had a nickname because he had never shared it with his colleagues during his time in the force.

When I began to establish myself in the team, big Jim Easton was the regular centre half. He didn't half like a slide tackle. Forwards could always see Jim's tackles coming – they almost got a five minute warning. That didn't stop him winning the ball though. His tackles were usually perfectly timed and successful. Jim was great in the air as well. It was a shame when he broke his leg and Hibs let him move to Dundee when he was fit again. He did a great job at Dens Park. I saw Jim recently; he was in charge of a touring party of Native American Indians and he had taken them for a visit to the Hibs Supporters Club. As you do, of course.

After Jock Stein took over at Easter Road in March 1964, one of the first things he did was to sign a centre half. Jock believed a team should have a strong spine and the man he selected to provide backbone to Hibs was John McNamee. He couldn't have chosen better. Being ahead of his time, Stein also decided to play with a 4–2–4 system and he picked me to partner John at the back.

Big Mac was a man mountain. He was physically imposing and intimidating in equal measure. He didn't just put the fear of God into his opponents, he could frighten his team mates as well. Mostly placid off the park, John was the complete opposite when he crossed the white line. Although he was very much an uncompromising centre half, John had a bit of football in him as well. He was one of the first goal scoring centre halves and he used to go forward for every corner or free kick. The problem was that he took his time in getting back afterwards. I would shout at him to hurry up but he just ignored me. If I tried again, he gave me a look that said it all. After getting a couple of these looks, I didn't try any more.

John had his problems with referees and was sent off on a few occasions. One referee who always seemed to be pointing him towards the dressing room was a Mr Crawley. Maybe he didn't like the big man or maybe it was just coincidence. When we played Celtic in the League Cup semi final at Ibrox in 1965, we were forced into a replay because Celtic scored an equaliser in the last minute of the first game. Early in the second match, John was sent off for a tackle on John Hughes. I think it's fair to say that he considered the decision unjust. He was only persuaded to leave the field with difficulty. As he approached the tunnel, he had a change of heart, turned round and made for the referee. I ran over to try to stop him. I grabbed hold of him but he just kept on going with me hanging on to his back. Fortunately, he saw sense and decided to leave the pitch. As he passed the Celtic bench, he kicked the dugout ferociously. Masonry flew everywhere. He then disappeared up the tunnel. Neil Mochan was sitting on that bench and he told me years later that the whole incident had been 'quite frightening'.

John was not a great admirer of Rangers. He relished matches against them and always produced his best. If we had played Rangers every week, Big Mac would have been regarded as the best centre half in the world. One of his greatest games was at Ibrox when we won 4–2 just three days after beating Real Madrid at Easter Road. John was outstanding in both of these games and proved that he could be disciplined when he wanted.

John was an interesting character off the field too. In those days, players didn't use deodorants or body sprays. The nearest you got to male grooming was a sprinkle of Tom McNiven the physio's talcum powder. John used to have young children and would regularly help himself to a couple of tins of Tom's talc. Tom would always complain about this after John went home.

One of the boys said to Tom one day, 'Why don't you talk to him about it?'

Tom replied, 'Why do you think I don't talk to him about it?'

You didn't argue with Mac. If we were playing cards on the train on the way to an away game and he was losing, he would just pick up the cards and throw them out of the window. Once on a pre-season tour to the Highlands, Jimmy O'Rourke, Pat Quinn and I were listening to music in the hotel lounge. John turned to us and told us to switch the record player off. Of course, we did and very quickly too! Later, I plucked up the courage to ask the big man why he had made us turn off the music when we were enjoying it.

His answer was straight to the point: 'I liked the tune but I didnae like the words.'

When he retired, John became a postman. I don't think too many dogs would have barked at him. Most of the time, he was a genuinely nice big man though, and he was a top class centre half. He was commanding in the air and rock hard on the ground and his physical presence concentrated the minds of every centre forward he came up against. They say that good players produce their best against the best and John certainly did that against Real Madrid.

However, that match against Real Madrid stands out in my mind not just because of John's outstanding performance. Since this was such a special game, Bill Harrower, our chairman, decided that we should wear a different strip. Earlier in the week, Jock Stein asked Jimmy O'Rourke and me to model the chairman's choice of kit for him. He had chosen a combination of our normal green and white top with red shorts.

Actually it didn't look too bad but Jimmy wasn't for it. 'We're surely no playing Real Madrid with red shorts on are we boss?' he asked Stein.

When the chairman left, Stein answered Jimmy's question with two of his own. He said, 'Does the chairman want a change of strip tomorrow?' and followed up with, 'What are Hibs' traditional colours?'

The next night Hibs wore green shorts for the first time. They looked great and we played great. The manager had kept the chairman happy by changing the strip, yet also kept the fans and players happy by choosing the right colours. That was big Jock, always thinking, usually right.

I was playing at sweeper at that time and I have to say that I found it an easy position to play. The whole game was in front of you and you could read the play and make your interceptions and tackles. Sometimes you didn't even need to do that as you were just picking up the opposition's misplaced passes. I used to get a round of applause from the crowd for just collecting an over-hit pass and knocking it back to Willie Wilson. I remember thinking that it couldn't be bad when you got a clap for passing the ball back to the keeper. The hardest part of playing sweeper was making good use of the ball to start a counter attack. That came naturally to me though, and I didn't find it difficult.

I had the occasional game at centre half as well. One such game was the 1968 League Cup semi final against Dundee at Tynecastle. Their centre forward was big George McLean, a good player and a real character. He put them in front, ran into the net, then picked up the ball and carried it back to the centre circle. As he passed me, he said, 'The big man's done it again.'

I didn't normally get angry on the park but his cockiness riled me. I chased after him and told him simply, 'We'll beat you.' We did beat them through a last minute goal from Alan McGraw. Alan had injured his knee badly earlier in the game but had bravely stayed on and his goal poacher's instincts saw him in the right place at the right time to poke home the winner.

As soon as the final whistle blew, I headed straight for McLean. He literally held his hands up and said, 'All right, all right, you deserved it.' Big Dandy, as McLean was known, was one of football's nice guys but you could never have called him shy.

When John McNamee left for Newcastle, centre forwards throughout Scotland probably breathed a big sigh of relief, but his successor was no soft touch either. Bob Shankly signed the Dane John Madsen from Morton. He was small, stocky, blond, bullet headed and as hard as nails. Very little went past him but he did disappoint me on one occasion.

We had gone to Cappielow to play his old club. Morton had a centre forward at that time called 'Sugar' Osborne. He was a part time player and had got his nickname from his day job, which was driving a lorry for Tate and Lyle. Sugar liked to put himself about and he certainly did so that day. John Madsen was visibly upset by his roughhouse tactics and said to Bob Shankly at half time, 'What he's doing to me is not right.' That surprised me because Madsen was normally happy to give and take punishment on the field. He did well for Hibs though, and we were sorry to see him go when he decided to go back to Denmark to take up his previous career as a draughtsman again.

Jim Black had been a solid reliable centre half for Airdrie for quite a few seasons when we signed him. He was to be a fixture in Eddie Turnbull's great Tornadoes team, of course, but he was always quiet and understated. He was a really good player for Hibs and his contribution was never fully appreciated. He preferred to mark a centre forward who played up close to him and he usually came out on top against that type of player. One player who caused him all sorts of bother though was Dixie Deans of Celtic who scored a lot of goals against us. The problem that Jim had with Deans was handling his mobility. Dixie was never still and always on the prowl and Jim found that hard to cope with.

I liked big Cilla on and off the field. He was difficult to rouse normally but got a bit annoyed one night in Norway. We were playing Trondheim and their centre forward kept battering into Jim. Jim told him to stop it but he carried on. I then heard his voice saying, 'Right that's it. I've had enough.' The next time the ball came into our box, Jim headed it clear and everyone including the referee followed the direction of the ball. I heard a thumping noise behind me and turned to see the centre forward lying in a heap on the ground. Jim simply said, 'Well, I did tell him.' That was the way big Lanarkshire lads settled things. The centre played the rest of the game on the right wing giving Jim Black as wide a berth as possible.

Cilla's long-standing central defensive partner was John Blackley. When John broke through into the team, I moved to midfield where I enjoyed playing. Apart from anything else, it gave me the chance to score a few goals.

John was a top player and a great Hibee. He read the game brilliantly, tackled superbly, won his headers and was a terrific user of the ball. I remember when John joined up at Easter Road, he was one of a group of talented young players. John outstripped the lot of them though because as well as having ability, he had a desire to succeed and a strong competitive instinct. He wasn't scared of hard work either. John always made his opinions known on the pitch. He was constantly at his team mates, his opponents, the referee and the linesman. Nobody escaped.

A game against Rangers at Ibrox sticks in my mind. It was a close match and whoever scored next was clearly going to win. Rangers scored an offside goal. It was miles offside and everybody in the ground could see it except for the linesman. John let his passions boil to the surface and headed for the official. He proceeded to tell him exactly what he thought of him and I can tell you that his opinion of the flag carrier in question was not at all complimentary. As captain, I tried to reason with John but he was too far gone. I told him that if he didn't walk away he would be sent off. That was one of my more accurate forecasts. In no time at all, John, still seething, was heading for the tunnel. Now we were unjustly a goal behind and we were also a man down. Unfair? Definitely, but that was life when you visited Ibrox or Parkhead.

When I was manager, I brought John back as my assistant.

We were struggling at that time and I soon realised that he was still the best sweeper at the club. I asked him to get his boots back on and he did with great success. Even in his mid thirties, as he was by then, he was top drawer. Aberdeen under Alex Ferguson was the top team in Scotland at that time. We beat them 2–1 at Easter Road one day. Willie Irvine got both our goals and although they had Alex McLeish and Willie Miller in central defence, John was the best defender on the field by a mile.

John was a great player with a ruthless streak and he carried that ruthlessness into management when he succeeded me as Hibs boss. As a manager, you deal with a variety of players who are all different types of people. Some of them are dedicated professionals while others are rascals. You wouldn't invite them all home for a dinner but you have to work with every one of them. If a player will do it for you on the park on a Saturday then you should pick him whether he's your cup of tea or not. I am not sure if John always did that as a manager. He was a wonderful player though.

When Eddie Turnbull decided that he wanted a more physical presence at centre half than Jim Black provided, he went to Coventry City and signed big Roy Barry. Roy had played for Hearts and Dunfermline before going down south and had done a great job for both clubs. He was big, rugged and hard as nails on the park but had a taste for the finer things in life off it. He wore expensive clothes, was widely read, ate in gourmet restaurants and considered himself to be a connoisseur of fine wines. This was at a time, remember, when most of his team mates had difficulty telling export from lager.

On the field though, Roy was a different person. When we played against Morton at Cappielow, Roy came up against Sugar Osborne who had upset as hard a player as John Madsen only a few years earlier. Sugar didn't worry big Roy. Quite the reverse. Roy hit him with a couple of trademark tackles early on and Osborne kept his distance for the rest of the match. Roy was a character of contrasts. I always thought of him as a sophisticated desperado.

Big George Stewart joined Hibs not long before I left for Celtic. We were jogging round the track one morning shortly after he had arrived and he asked me what life at Easter Road was like. I told him that as a Hibs fanatic himself he would love it. 'Mind you,' I added, 'make sure that you get them on your side,' and I pointed up to the section of the North Stand where the most raucous supporters used to sit. A lot of players had found over the years that if you didn't get that group of fans on your side then life with Hibs could be tough. That never proved a problem for George though, as the crowd took to him from the start.

George was big, strong, enthusiastic and a great motivator as captain. He was a top class, all round defender and probably came to Hibs just a little late in his career. A lot of people have said that if Eddie Turnbull had signed George earlier, the Tornadoes might have won more trophies. They might be right but we'll never know.

George was on my backroom staff when I was manager and along with Jimmy O'Rourke, he was a great help to me. I remember one Saturday when George, Jimmy Thomson our coach and I decided to go up to Aberdeen to watch the Dons playing Ipswich. We drove to Kirkcaldy in Jimmy's car and took the train from there. We had intended to come straight back after the game but ended up staying in Aberdeen for the night. When we got back to Kirkcaldy on the Sunday, Jimmy's car wouldn't start. While I was giving him a push, George disappeared in the general direction of the shops. By the time he came back, Jimmy had the engine running and we were ready to go. George jumped in holding a white carrier bag.

We asked him what was in it and he took out a frozen chicken.

When we asked him what that was all about, he informed us that after his unexpected overnight stay in Aberdeen, he would need a peace offering for his wife and that's what the chicken was. When Jimmy asked, 'But why a frozen chicken?' George replied that the butcher's shop had been the first he had come to. 'In that case,' said Jimmy, 'it's a good job that the first shop in the street wasn't a hardware store.'

On another occasion, George, Jimmy and I went out for an Italian meal. The proprietor of the restaurant had employed a guitarist to walk round the tables serenading the customers. This was going down better with some diners than others. It was really annoying Jimmy who was trying to talk to George and me about football. When the musician returned to our table, Jimmy positively bristled. He got to this feet and pointed his finger at the man. He said, 'I want a word with you.' George and I feared the worst but Jimmy merely said, 'Do you know any Beatles songs?' We breathed a sigh of relief and carried on with our meal.

During my spell as manager, I was lucky to have Gordon Rae as my centre half. Gordon had started as a forward, moved back to midfield and then found his best position at centre half. He had a tremendous build, was good in the air and had a terrific shot in him. Gordon also had a big heart. He gave you everything. I heard it said that Gordon had started life as a Hearts supporter. Well it never showed when he pulled on a green jersey. He had some of his best games against Hearts. When we beat them in the Scottish Cup quarter final in 1979, Gordon scored a great goal with one of his rockets and George Stewart headed the other. I remember Gordon getting sent off at Tynecastle on the day when Stevie Archibald scored a classic striker's goal. We really missed Gordon when he was suspended and couldn't play in the 1985 League Cup

Final against Aberdeen and he thoroughly deserved the testimonial match against Manchester United that he was awarded by the club.

George Stewart and Kenny McLean were on Gordon's organising committee and they asked me right at the start if I would approach Alex Ferguson and ask him if Manchester United would do the honours for big Gordon. I gave Alex a ring and he invited Kenny, George and me down to Old Trafford for the next home game. He met us before the game and asked us just one question: 'Has he played for anybody else other than Hibs?' Kenny assured Alex that Gordon had spent his whole professional career to that point at Easter Road. 'You've got your testimonial then,' said Alex.

It was a tremendous gesture and one that Gordon really appreciated. A bumper crowd turned out for the match, which unfortunately was spoiled as a contest early on when George Smith, the referee, sent off Joe Tortolano for a reckless tackle on Gordon Strachan. The referee could have asked Hibs to substitute Tortolano and kept the sides even but he didn't and the game suffered as a result. Mind you, Joe should really have known better.

Having brought his team all the way north out of the goodness of his heart, Alex Ferguson wasn't pleased to see his star midfielder being kicked. Wee Strachan wouldn't have been too happy either.

When I was at Aberdeen with Fergie, we always found little Gordon to be a man with strong views. If you asked him a question, he would never give you a straight 'yes' or 'no'. He always had to have something to say for himself. He's the same as a manager, as is one of his former Pittodrie colleagues Mark McGhee. It's always good to hear a manager's thoughts on a game but we don't need philosophers and we don't need to be lectured. Some of today's managers should bear that in mind.

Jackie McNamara regularly partnered both George Stewart and Gordon Rae in central defence. Jackie was a great player for Hibs. He came in exchange for me, of course. I had no idea that the deal was in the offing. Eddie Turnbull had gone off me at that time and I have never really found out why that was the case. He telephoned me out of the blue one day and said gruffly, 'Here's Mr Stein to talk to you.' Jock Stein wanted to take me to Parkhead and although it wasn't a career move that I was looking for, it turned out to be a good one for me.

Jackie's switch to Hibs worked out well too. Once he got his knee injuries fixed, he gave the club great service over many years. He was a top player who read the game well and was an expert at organising his defence. Jackie was a man of strong opinions and he was never slow to express them. I liked that in him.

When Alan Rough played behind Jackie and big Rae, he would mostly leave them to deal with high balls into the box. One day, as Jackie was preparing to head the ball away, Alan came racing off his line and punched the ball clear. He clattered into Jackie and flattened him in the process. When Jackie picked himself up, he looked at Roughie and said, 'But you never come for crosses.'

In his usual likeable but eccentric way, big Alan replied, 'Aye you're right Jackie. I never come for crosses.'

Jackie didn't score many goals but he got one in my biggest ever win as Hibs manager. When we beat Kilmarnock 8–1, Jackie chipped in with a goal. Hibs would have been in a sorry state in the late seventies and early eighties without players like George Stewart, Gordon Rae, Ralph Callachan, Jackie McNamara and Ally McLeod.

Hibs unearthed yet another top centre half when Craig Paterson followed his dad John to Easter Road. Tall and commanding on the park and confident and articulate off it, Craig was always going places. The place he eventually went to was Ibrox but we got good money for him and I always thought that Craig played his best football when he was at Hibs.

I signed Gordon Hunter for Hibs and there's a wee story attached to that. Gordon was on an S Form and was still at school and training part time. One day, I was sitting in the dressing room on my own after training and Gordon came in. I asked him why he wasn't at school and he told me that he had just left. Without thinking, I asked him what kind of career he had in mind. He blushed a bit and said, 'Well, I'd quite like to join the ground staff here.' As soon as it dawned on me that we could now sign Gordon on a proper contract, I took him down to the secretary's office and got the business done without delay.

A great bit of business it proved to be. Gordon had pace and was a tremendous tackler. He and Willie Miller played in the same back four and were two of the hardest tacklers I've ever seen. Off the field, Gordon was a quiet lad but on it, he would kick you as soon as look at you. When Geebsie stiffened someone, he just walked away. He never bothered with going through the motions of pretending that he hoped his opponent was okay. His job as a defender was to let forwards know that he was around and he excelled at that.

Gordon Hunter and Tommy McIntyre formed a terrific partnership at the heart of Hibs' defence when we won the Skol League Cup in 1991. Alex Miller had originally played McIntyre at full back but it hadn't worked. He was much more comfortable at centre half and did a great job there in tandem with Geebsie.

Tommy was an expert penalty taker as well and he scored the crucial opening goal against Dunfermline from the spot in the Skol Cup Final. Taking penalties can be nerve wracking.

I know because I scored them and missed them in my time. The best way to approach taking a penalty is to think purely about scoring and not let the possibility of missing enter your mind. It's when you do that that you've got problems. Tommy was always confident and focused and his record from the spot was pretty good.

Stephen Tweed displaced Tommy and did well before he went off to Greece under freedom of contract. He ended up playing for quite a few clubs but he is back in Scotland now as manager of Montrose. He is a big guy with a fair bit of self-belief and could do well as a manager although he hasn't made the best of starts at Links Park.

Jocky Scott brought John Hughes to Hibs during his short-term stint as manager after Alex Miller left. Like George Stewart before him, Yogi came to Hibs late in his career but he was a massive presence and influence both on the pitch and in the dressing room. Yogi had a sense of fun but approached the game with an underlying seriousness. He had a real will to win and no centre forward liked playing against him. To me, he was always a manager in the making and it'll be interesting to see how he fares in the hot seat at Easter Road.

Yogi quite often partnered Shaun Dennis at Hibs and they were a pair of mighty men. Shaun did a great job for Hibs in their promotion season. He was a stand-out for Raith Rovers in the First Division as well and that was the level that probably suited him best.

When Alex McLeish decided to convert Franck Sauzée into a sweeper after he had spent most of his career in midfield, it was a masterstroke. Sauzée had a definite aura of greatness. He seemed to have so much time on the ball, which is always a sign of a top player. He read the game brilliantly, got himself into the right place for his interceptions and made his tackles when he had to. Most of all, he used the ball superbly. Franck made his team mates better players. His searching passes took players into attacking positions that they might not have gone into of their own accord. He was the perfect example to any young player.

I really liked Franck's attitude. As a class player with a worldwide reputation, he could have come to Hibs to wind his career down and pick up some easy money. He never did that. Nothing demonstrated his commitment to Hibs better than the headed goal he scored against Hearts at Easter Road. Sauzée went for that header knowing that a clash of heads was likely. He took the knock and lost a few teeth in the process but the ball ended up in the Hearts net. When Franck came to, he shook his head, got back into position and played out the rest of the game.

He wasn't just committed to Hibs on the park, he bought into the club's culture and tradition as well. I remember meeting him at a function in the North Stand and he was wearing a kilt in the Hibs tartan. The fans loved him and rightly so. It's just a shame that he didn't make it when he moved into the manager's chair. He didn't get very long in charge, of course, but the early signs weren't good. Franck's English wasn't perfect but then again neither is my French. His lack of total fluency in English probably didn't help him. His biggest handicap as manager though was that he didn't have himself as a player. When Franck Sauzée stopped playing to concentrate on managing, the heart and a lot of the quality went out of the Hibs team.

Probably Franck's best signing at Hibs was Gary Caldwell. Caldwell had a couple of spells with us and was a good player who was never short on self-confidence. The fans turned against him when he signed a pre-contract agreement with Celtic but I thought that he kept his head up well and did his best for us for the rest of that season.

It was Tony Mowbray who signed Rob Jones and it was a top signing. I've got a lot of time for big Jonesy. He played to his strengths and held our defence together for three seasons. Chris Hogg made huge strides as a player when he formed a partnership with Jones. Rob was six foot seven and some really tall men are not as good in the air as you would expect them to be. He was very good indeed. He won his headers and got the ball well out of the box. When he learned to stay in the centre and not get dragged out wide, which he did very quickly, he was extremely effective. He was a real threat in the other team's box as well and got his fair share of goals. There was none better, of course, than his header against Kilmarnock in the 2007 CIS League Cup Final. He showed that he could score with his feet too in the quarter final win over Hearts.

When I met Rob, I liked him as a man. He was an impressive character and that helped make him a good captain. He was put in a difficult position by some of his colleagues during the revolt against John Collins leading up to the 2007 Scottish Cup semi final against Dunfermline but came through it to give us great service. We got three good years from Rob Jones and made a profit when we sold him. He always showed Hibs total respect and is guaranteed a deservedly warm welcome if he ever returns to Easter Road.

Mixu Paatelainen signed Sol Bamba and he was definitely one of Mixu's better acquisitions. Sol stands tall and confident and has a real presence. He's got a lot of skill for a big man too. He never hides and is prepared to take responsibility in tough games when some of his team mates are looking for an easy way out.

Sol is a regular for the Ivory Coast now and when he's away on international duty with the likes of Didier Drogba and Kolo Toure, he'll be having his eyes opened by how much more than him these guys are earning. If Sol maintains his form, a big move could be his for the taking. We'll see. One thing's for sure though. Whoever buys him will have to pay a lot more to secure his services than Hibs handed over to Dunfermline when we signed him.

I've thought long and hard about who the centre halves in my dream team should be. It didn't take me long to narrow my choice down to three players but that's when my difficulties started. Picking two from my top three was really hard. My short list is John McNamee, John Blackley and Franck Sauzée.

It really depends on what sort of defensive pairing I'm looking for. Alex Ferguson's Manchester United team has a blend in central defence in Nemanja Vidic and Rio Ferdinand. Vidic is the hard tackling ball winner who dominates in the air while Ferdinand reads the game, makes interceptions and starts moves.

In the great Liverpool team that Bob Paisley built in the seventies and eighties, both centre halves, Alan Hansen and Mark Lawrenson, were footballers. They could defend but they were comfortable on the ball and were able to carry it forward and counter attack.

If I was going for the first of these set-ups, I would definitely choose John McNamee. Big Mac would win everything in the air and crunch into his tackles. No centre forward would enjoy playing against him.

However, I think that I prefer Bob Paisley's approach. John Blackley and Franck Sauzée would give me two footballing centre halves in perfect partnership. They would know who to pick up, when to stay and when to move forward. They would be able to make their tackles and win their headers, and their reading of a game is second to none. Most of all they are capable of turning defence into attack by linking with their midfield or by making a short or long defence-splitting pass.

What a combination these two would make. They were both footballers of the highest class and Franck brings the added bonus of goal scoring. He fired in tremendous free kick goals for Hibs and I want as many of my outfield players as possible to offer me the option of a few goals every season.

So, with apologies to Big McNamee, and I'll definitely take cover next time I see him, I'm going for Sauzée and Blackley. I'm delighted with my choice and my team is really starting to take shape. Now I'm moving to the midfield and if my selection task was hard before, it's about to become almost impossible. Hibs have had so many great wingers and central midfield players that I really do have an embarrassment of riches as I move on to the middle section of my dream team.

CO-AUTHOR'S NOTE

Pat and I have taken a consistent approach to the writing of this book. We have looked at each area of the team in turn and started with a discussion of all the Hibs players in that position whom Pat has watched or played with during his lifetime. We have then drawn up a short list of those who have made the greatest contribution. Pat's memories and opinions of the short-listed players form the basis of each chapter.

This chapter on central defenders was no different. When Pat made his final choice, I threw a question at him. I asked him whether he wanted to be considered for his dream team as a central defender or a midfielder. Being the modest man that he is, Pat said that he would be happy to leave himself out altogether.

I told him that he was one of Hibs' greatest ever players and had to be included. I said, 'Pat, you are a genuine living legend and if we didn't have you in the final team, there would be a riot.' After some persuasion, Pat agreed to be included in the team. We then debated whether Pat should be selected at the back or in midfield. After some consideration, Pat opted for a place in the back four as he had enjoyed playing there more and found it an easier position to occupy.

This meant that the midfield was going to be deprived of a truly great player. Pat estimates that he played two thirds of his games for Hibs in central midfield. He was an outstanding performer there. He always seemed to have time to spare on the ball, which is of course the mark of a great player. When I mentioned this to Pat, he recalled a conversation he had had with Duncan Falconer early in his career at Hibs. Pat had remarked to Falconer that he found he had very little time on the ball now that he had stepped up into first team football. Falconer told Pat not to worry and assured him that the time on the ball he was looking for would come with experience. He then added with his tongue firmly in his cheek, 'Unless you get freed first.'

There was no chance of Hibs ever freeing Pat Stanton and that time on the ball certainly did become a part of Pat's game as his career progressed. He was an imperious player who was always composed. Nothing flustered Pat. He read the game superbly and tackled like the true defender he was. He anticipated and intercepted brilliantly, made accurate and, when necessary, incisive passes and scored a lot of goals. Quite a few of these goals were with headers because Pat was excellent in the air. If Pat's own estimate of the number of games he played in midfield is correct, he probably played around 450 times in the centre of the park. In those games he scored eighty-three goals, which is a ratio of almost one goal in every five games.

This is a phenomenal output for a midfield player but Pat

was no ordinary player. In all, he played nearly 700 games for Hibs and many of his performances were memorable. If I had to choose the best game that Pat played for our club, I would have no hesitation in nominating the 1972 League Cup Final against Celtic. Hibs won 2–1 and Pat scored the first goal, made the second for Jimmy O'Rourke and hit the post for good measure. He was truly immense that day and Celtic just couldn't cope with him. I had first watched Pat play at Holy Cross Academy in the late nineteen fifties. I played for the first year team and as soon as we finished our match, we changed quickly and hurried back out to watch the school's top team in action. As well as Pat, Jimmy O'Rourke and Davie Hogg were members of that same team who went on to play for Hibs. It was obvious watching Pat even then that he was a class apart. He was clearly destined for a great career in football. In my view that glittering career reached a peak on a cold day in December 1972 at Hampden Park when Pat showed Celtic's greatest ever team how to play football.

All of the above is a testimony to how good a midfield player Pat Stanton was. Yet Pat considers himself to have been even better in central defence. How good must he have been at the back then? The answer is better than the best. When Tommy Docherty became Scotland manager, he selected Pat as sweeper and declared, 'Pat Stanton is better than Bobby Moore.' Moore had captained England to World Cup glory in 1966 and had played the game of his life against Pelé and his great Brazilian team in the 1970 World Cup in Mexico. By common consent, he was the best central defender in world football.

Yet when the Doc made his statement, very few people north of the border argued with him. Certainly no Hibs fan took issue with the Scotland boss's bold statement. We knew how good Pat was in central defence. In 1964 when he had just turned twenty, Pat played sweeper in the Hibs team that beat Real Madrid 2–0 at Easter Road. His performance was superlative. He was so commanding that night that the great Ferenc Puskás kicked him in frustration.

Pat was majestic at the back. He would step in, win the ball and carry it forward in that graceful style of his and start another move. Younger readers wanting to visualise how Pat played the game in central defence should know that he had a similarly elegant style to players like Alan Hansen and Rio Ferdinand. He was much better in the air than either of those two though. He could tackle harder as well.

Pat and I decided then that he would come into his own Hibernian Dream Team as a central defender. The next major decision was to choose who would partner Pat. This meant that one of either John Blackley or Franck Sauzée, Pat's two original choices, had to give way.

John Blackley was a magnificent player for Hibs who also earned Scotland caps. The very fact that Pat agreed to move to midfield in Hibs' team to accommodate Blackley shows how good John was. I watched Blackley during his initial Hibs career and I took my children to watch him play when he came back to Hibs in the early eighties as Player/Assistant Manager. They were young then but they knew class when they saw it and John Blackley had that particular commodity in abundance.

It can't be denied though that Franck Sauzée was something special. Franck had won a lot of caps for a top international team like France and had won the European Cup with Marseilles. He arrived at Easter Road when Hibs were suffering the indignity of playing to win promotion out of the First Division. Along with Russell Latapy, he revolutionised our team and galvanised our club. Franck bought into the culture of Hibernian Football Club one hundred per cent and gave us supporters our pride in our team back. Initially, he played magnificently in midfield and scored some great goals. Two of the best of these came against Hearts and were all the sweeter for that. He really excelled though when he moved back to sweeper.

As I have said, John Blackley was class. At his peak, however, Franck Sauzée was world class, and that is the difference. After much heart searching, Pat eventually decided to choose Franck Sauzée to partner him in central defence in his dream team. It was a matter of great regret to Pat that he had to leave out his long time friend and team mate John Blackley but he felt that the claims of the great Sauzée just could not be overlooked.

Ted Brack

4

WONDERS ON THE WING

When I came into professional football, every team played with two wingers. These attacking players operated out wide and were makers and takers of goals. Nowadays, of course, the winger is an endangered species. There are not too many of them around but those who are on the scene are dangerous players who can make things happen. Many teams in modern football flood their midfield and pack their defence and it is really hard to create chances. If you try to go through the centre of a crowded defence, the odds are that your move will break down. That means that you have to go round the outside and that's where wingers come in.

Even in today's game, players like Aiden McGeady and Aaron Lennon go past players, hit the goal line and set up goals for their team mates. In recent years, Ryan Giggs and Cristiano Ronaldo have won many games for Manchester United and in the sixties and seventies, no team in Scotland really managed to get to grips with either Willie Henderson of Rangers or Jimmy Johnstone of Celtic.

The fifties was the golden age of wingers though. England had Stanley Matthews and Tom Finney and Hibs had Gordon Smith and Willie Ormond. Jimmy Greaves, the legendary Tottenham and England striker, paid Smith the ultimate compliment. Greavsie wrote that Gordon could dribble like

Matthews and shoot like Finney. That's some accolade but one which Gordon Smith thoroughly deserved.

I grew up in a Hibs supporting household where our right winger was revered. It's hardly surprising since we are talking about a man who scored a hat trick against Hearts on his debut in green and white and, five months later, starred in an 8–1 win over Rangers at Easter Road.

When I made my home debut for Hibs in 1963, our opponents were Dundee. By that time, Gordon Smith was a Dundee player. Hibs had been careless enough to release him thinking that his best days were behind him. Gordon signed for Hearts and led them to the League Championship. After two years at Tynecastle he moved on again to Dens Park. Another League Championship followed and Gordon ended up with five league winners' medals. Three of them, of course, came from his days at Hibs when he and his Famous Five colleagues reigned supreme in Scottish football.

Anyway, I made my way on to the park at Easter Road that day in great trepidation. I was playing left half and lined up quite close to Gordon at the start of the game. I looked at him in sheer awe and he responded like the nice man he was by smiling at me. It was the only time in my life that I was intimidated by a smile but intimidated I most certainly was. Being on the same park as Gordon Smith was like playing cowboys with John Wayne.

Gordon was nearly forty by this time and understandably was not as quick as he once had been. He was really graceful, stronger than I expected and a great crosser of the ball. He caused me quite a few problems in the first half. In the dressing room at half time, our manager Walter Galbraith told me to kick Gordon in the second half. I just shook my head and said to him, 'How can you ask me to kick Gordon Smith? If I did that I would never be allowed back in my house. My dad would be waiting at the door with my suitcase packed.'

Dundee won that game 4–1. They had a great team at that time with players like Alex Hamilton and Ian Ure in defence, Andy Penman in midfield and Alan Gilzean up front. Hamilton was quite a character. He used to hand the winger he was up against a complimentary ticket before the game and tell him to go and sit in the stand. 'You'd be as well to,' he'd say, 'because you're not going to get a kick of the ball today.'

One man stood out though, in that team of many talents, and that man was Gordon Smith. When Gordon got the ball, his opponents used to line three or four players up in wait for him. They took it for granted that he would beat the first man and they would need reinforcements. When I got home after that game my dad reminded me that I had been in the presence of greatness. 'You'll not experience that every week,' he said. 'The man you were playing against today wasn't just any player. He was Gordon Smith.'

I got to know Gordon after he retired. He was clean living, exuded good health and was a very modest man. When you spoke to him he made you feel good about yourself. I was invited once to a presentation to Stewart Brown who covered Hibs games for the Evening News for many years. It was held at the old Fifties Club opposite the main stand at Easter Road. Everybody who was anybody was there. One of the organisers came up to me and asked if I would make the presentation to Stewart and say a few words. I pointed over to the corner of the room where Gordon Smith was sitting and asked, 'Why would you want to ask Dean Martin when Frank Sinatra is sitting in the corner?'

In the fifties, the Partick Thistle goalkeeper John Fairbairn earned himself a reputation for saving penalties. Mind you, I am sure that he didn't save as many as Ronnie Simpson did for Hibs. Anyway, Arthur Montford on Scotsport asked if goalkeepers should really be able to save penalties on a regular basis. This sparked off a bit of a debate and Scotsport arranged a challenge which involved Gordon Smith going through to Firhill to take penalties against Fairbairn. Gordon not only scored every one but he told Fairbairn which corner of the net he was putting the ball in before he hit each shot.

Gordon lived in North Berwick. I remember we were training down there one day and a Porsche quietly drew up at the side of the training pitch. In it was Gordon Smith. One of the young players didn't recognise him and said to me, 'Somebody's watching us.'

I said, 'That's not just somebody son. That's one of the greatest players who has ever lived.' When Gordon saw us looking at him, he started his engine and drove away. At heart, he was a quiet and very unassuming man.

When Stan Mortenson played for Blackpool and England in the fifties, he once scored a hat trick for England in a midweek international. On the Friday, his manager Joe Smith put up the team sheets for the weekend games. Mortenson's name wasn't on any of the team lists. When he asked his manager why he had been left out of all the club's teams the weekend after scoring a hat trick for his country, Stan was taken aback to be told, 'To be honest with you son, I just forgot all about you.' That would never have happened to Gordon Smith. He was a truly unforgettable footballer.

Gordon Smith's wing partner was Willie Ormond. Willie was small, direct and dangerous. His right foot was only for standing on but his left was so good that it didn't matter. He survived serious injuries which might have finished some players and was still being picked for Scotland as late as 1959. He carried on playing for Hibs into the early sixties and played in the famous win over Barcelona. He could always be relied on to score his fair share of goals and he could make them as well.

Lawrie Reilly still tells me today that Gordon Smith and Willie Ormond made goal scoring easy for him by the quality of their crosses. When Lawrie retired, Gordon and Willie laid on a few goals for the young Joe Baker as well.

Willie became a manager when he retired and took St Johnstone into Europe. He's so well thought of in Perth that they've called one of their stands after him. He went on to manage Scotland. I played for him against West Germany in Frankfurt. Erich Schaedler played in that game as well. Willie was a really nice man, which is not something you can say about a lot of managers, and he had great ideas on the game.

When Willie moved on to Falkirk at the end of his career, Hibs found another great winger in wee Johnny McLeod. Johnny could play on either wing. He was fast and tricky and soon got chosen for Scotland. Unfortunately, his first cap was against England at Wembley in 1961 and as every Scot knows but wants to forget, England won 9–3.

McLeod played junior football with Joe Baker at Armadale Thistle. By the time they moved to Hibs they had developed quite a combination. When Joe moved to Torino, Johnny went to Arsenal. A year later they were back together when Joe was transferred to Highbury.

McLeod did well at Highbury before moving on to Aston Villa. During his time at Villa Park, he was joined by Willie Hamilton. Johnny did his best to keep Willie on the straight and narrow. McLeod and Hamilton lived close to each other. One Saturday morning Willie phoned Johnny to say that he needed a bit of help to get ready for the game. When McLeod went round to Hamilton's house, it was obvious that he was in a bad way. Willie had clearly had a heavy Friday night and hadn't quite recovered from it. Johnny got him into a cold shower, filled him with black coffee and then drove him to the ground. Willie kept his head down and was able to stop his manager from realising the fragile state that he was in. Needless to say, when the game started he was brilliant and ended up being voted man of the match.

When Hibs sold Johnny McLeod, they replaced him with a player who shared the same surname. Ally McLeod was signed from Blackburn Rovers. Yes, the same Ally who later won fame as an effervescent and successful club manager with Ayr and Aberdeen, and infamy after leading Scotland to their ill fated World Cup adventure in 1978.

Ally was a tricky left winger who had enjoyed a successful career in England with Blackburn, even playing in the 1960 FA Cup Final against Wolves. By the time he came to Hibs, his career was winding down. He ended up stepping back to midfield. He used his experience well there and even captained the club for a while. To say Ally was a character was a definite understatement. When he became manager of Ayr, he cut an extrovert figure in the technical area and was a constant source of copy for the football writers of the time.

We played Ayr at Somerset Park once and as usual, Ally was prowling the touchline. His assistant George Caldwell sat behind him on the bench. George was the complete opposite of Ally. You couldn't have met a quieter man. That day Ally was losing the plot as usual, roaring and bawling at the referee. Eventually the referee came across to Ally and was about to produce a card. Ally protested his innocence and pointed to his assistant sitting quietly in the dugout. 'It wisnae me, it wis him. He never shuts his mouth,' said Ally.

Incredibly, the referee believed him and headed across to the bench to caution Caldwell. As poor George sat there nonplussed, Ally theatrically put his finger to his lips and like a pantomime villain urged everyone round about to keep his secret. As he shook his head and muttered, 'Shush, shush,' I couldn't help but burst out laughing.

When Ally left Ayr to join Aberdeen as manager, his chairman told him that he should come to the boardroom after his last match. Ally duly did so expecting a valedictory speech and a presentation after the many years of service and success he had given to the club. The chairman called for quiet, turned to Ally and said simply, 'Ta Ta for noo.' Ally wasn't often stunned into silence but he was that day.

Jim Scott started his career at Hibs as a winger but ended it as a centre forward. When he played on the right wing, Jim was a great dribbler. He could beat men for fun and often left a trail of defenders behind him. He could score goals too. I remember one spectacular goal he got against Hearts at Tynecastle. He picked up the ball on the left touchline, cut inside past a defender and sent a rocket shot raging into the top of the net.

Jim also scored Hibs' only goal when we beat Berwick Rangers 1–0 in the Scottish Cup in 1967. Berwick had caused a sensation by knocking out Rangers in the previous round. They were managed by big Jock Wallace, who ironically was a Rangers man to the core. Wallace was promising a repeat of the previous round when Berwick came to Easter Road and there was a great crowd for the game. Nearly 30,000 fans were inside Easter Road that day and I said to Jimmy O'Rourke when we were warming up, 'How come so many people want to see Hibs play Berwick Rangers?'

Jimmy replied, 'They've come to see us get beat.' Well thanks to Jim Scott's goal, we didn't get beat.

I remember an amazing game when Jim got another important goal. We were playing Dunfermline at East End Park. Dunfermline were a top team in the sixties and it was really hard to go to their ground and win. We looked like doing it no bother that day. We went 4–0 up and when they came back to 4–2, we scored again. We should have been safe at 5–2 but we weren't; the Fifers kept fighting and pulled the score level at 5–5.

Alex Ferguson played up front for Dunfermline that day. Anybody who has seen Alex on the touchline at Old Trafford knows how much he likes to win. In the last minute he forced the ball over our line and then it was kicked clear. The referee waved play on and Fergie went ballistic. While all this was going on, we counter attacked and Jim Scott found himself one on one with the goalkeeper. Jim shot against the keeper's legs and the ball rebounded back off Jim and went into the net.

It was a lucky way to achieve a famous victory. You don't get many games finishing 6–5. Alex Ferguson probably still goes on about the goal he was denied to this day. He certainly never stopped mentioning it when we worked together at Aberdeen. I used to wind him up by saying, 'Alex, surely you know that the ref can't give a goal unless the ball actually hits the back of the net.' That used to make him even worse.

Jim Scott and I were chosen for a Scotland Select team to play Leicester City at Filbert Street. The match was a testimonial for Alex Dowdalls, the Leicester trainer who was now confined to a wheelchair. After the game, the Leicester chairman came into our dressing room and thanked us for our efforts on behalf of Mr Dowdalls. When he finished, Davie McParland, our captain, came over all sentimental and said, 'Mr Chairman, we'd like to donate our match fees to the testimonial fund.' The chairman thanked him profusely. This was a generous gesture by Davie but there was only one problem: he hadn't bothered to consult with the rest of us. We probably would have agreed but it would have been nice of him to ask.

Scotty was apoplectic. He was next to me and he was moaning his head off. His mood didn't improve when the chairman next presented us with small silver spoons with crests at the top. Jim turned to me and said in his broad Falkirk accent, 'We come all the way to Leicester and what have we got to show for it? A spin that's whit, a stupid wee silver spin!'

When Jim played on the right, Eric Stevenson was usually on the left. Eric was some player. I always thought of him as 'The Teddy Boy on the Wing' because of the massive quiff he had. Eric would shuffle up to full backs then leave them for dead. He could wrong foot defenders in his sleep.

I remember one game against Rangers when Bobby Shearer was right back for them. Bobby was a Scotland regular and one of the best in the business but Eric ran him ragged that day. Eric would run at Shearer, feint to go one way and then go the other, leaving the full back on the seat of his pants. It was a case of 'now you see it, now you don't'. It was one of Stevie's best ever games and there were plenty to choose from.

Eric won us a lot of penalties. Other teams accused him of diving. We just said that it was the wind behind the North Stand blowing him over. Joe Davis put away most of these penalties but Eric could never bear to look. He would look the other way until the crowd's roar told him that Joe had scored again.

Eric also had a pre-match superstition. He didn't like to have his boots checked before the game. When the referee came in to look over the studs, Eric used to hide in the toilet. You could see the ref looking around, thinking that someone was missing but not sure who it was. It was Eric and I never did ask him why he was so keen to avoid the boot inspection.

Eric was a great player though. He was a natural left winger but sometimes played on the right. When he did that he would cut in and shoot with his left foot. He was such an all round good player that he could play in midfield as well. That's where he played at Celtic Park on my twenty-fifth birthday when we won 2–1. Eric was up against Bobby Murdoch and Bertie Auld, two of the very best midfield players, and he played them off the park. It was a good birthday for me because I scored one of our goals and Johnny Hamilton got the other.

Eric was a talented player who was hugely underrated. He was exciting to watch, great to play with and difficult to play against. If he was playing now, he'd get at least fifty Scotland caps.

After Jim Scott left for Newcastle, Bob Shankly brought in his brother Alex from Everton. Alex had been a regular for Rangers and Scotland until wee Willie Henderson came on the scene. He lost his place to Willie and moved to Merseyside. He won the FA Cup with Everton before moving back to Scotland with us. Alex always seemed a bit more serious than his younger brother. Maybe he was just more mature.

He was a top player. He ran with his body crouched over the ball and he had terrific pace. His strength though was his crossing. It was first class. When we beat Napoli 5–0, Alex floated over a perfect corner for Peter Cormack to score the third goal and placed a great cross to the back post for me to head the fourth. Alex did well at Hibs but suffered a déjà vu experience. He had been a first team regular at Ibrox only to find himself displaced by a talented youngster. Now the same thing happened at Easter Road. Good though Alex was, he wasn't good enough to keep out Peter Marinello, who was just breaking through during Alex's time with us. Peter's form was such that he couldn't be held back any longer and Alex had to give way to him. It was a shame because Alex's class and experience brought something to our team, but Peter was playing so well that Bob Shankly just had to start selecting him.

Peter really started to make a name for himself when Willie MacFarlane became manager. There was nothing to him but he was a brave lad. Defenders dished out punishment to him on a regular basis but he always took it and came back for more. One of Peter's pre-match rituals was to leave changing until the last possible minute. He would be sitting there fully dressed at ten to three and then in no time at all he would slip into his strip and boots and be ready to go out with the rest of us at just after five to. Peter never bothered wearing shin pads, so with his socks at his ankles and his long hair he cut a distinctive figure.

He was really fast and had plenty of dribbling skill as well. He also got a few goals. His most famous goals were against Rangers at Ibrox. We went there in the autumn of 1969 as league leaders. We won 3–1 and Peter got two of them. He had a great game that day and really raised his profile. By Christmas, Hibs had sold him to Arsenal for £100,000 – a lot of money back then.

I think Peter would have been quite happy to stay at Hibs and he was taken aback at the speed with which his move to Highbury developed. I got a bit of a shock myself. The first I knew of it was when I turned on the teatime news on the television to hear it announced that Peter was away. I think Arsenal saw Marinello as London's answer to George Best and he made a great start down there. He couldn't keep it up though and, looking back, I think that such a big move came just a wee bit too early for Peter.

Having banked £100,000 for the sale of Peter Marinello, Hibs bought Arthur Duncan from Partick for £35,000. That turned out to be one of the best pieces of business the club has ever done. Arthur was brilliant for Hibs. He had the speed of a professional sprinter, could deliver a tremendous cross and scored his fair share of goals. He gave his all and played with a smile on his face. He was a real favourite with the fans.

He wasn't perfect mind you. He could be erratic. Some of his crosses were beauties. Others were a danger to the crowd behind the goals. He also had a habit of being caught offside. This used to drive Jimmy O'Rourke mad. Jimmy used to shout at Arthur to look across the line and keep himself onside. Arthur would reply, 'But I'm no offside all the time Jimmy.' Jimmy's reply was usually that the linesman clearly had a different opinion.

Arthur was such a nice lad that you couldn't stay angry with him for long. Everybody liked him. One of his best goals was our fifth in the 5–3 Drybrough Cup Final win over Celtic in 1972. Arthur outpaced Danny McGrain and hammered the ball home from what looked like an impossible angle. With Arthur, you always expected the unexpected. The element of surprise was always there with him. That was because Arthur usually had no idea what he was going to do next. If he didn't know, then what chance did the players marking him have of working out his intentions?

Arthur would approach the full back very slowly and then just accelerate past. When Arthur was away, there was no catching him. He was far too fast. He gave Hibs fantastic service over a long time and deserved the international caps that came his way. It's a shame that he'll probably be remembered for scoring the own goal that allowed Rangers to win the Scottish Cup in 1979 after two replays of the final.

Arthur's bad luck gave rise to a quiz question that is still doing the rounds. 'Which player played in three cup finals and scored the winning goal in the third but finished on the losing side?' The answer, of course, is Arthur but his misfortune on that night should never take away from his tremendous career with Hibs.

I don't think any Hibs player or supporter could really believe it when George Best signed for the club. Stewart Brown floated the idea of signing George in the Evening News and Tom Hart took him up on it. By the time George came to Easter Road, his best days were behind him but he was still some player. I had retired by then but the players who were still at the club used to tell me that George was a really nice man and that everybody at the club liked him.

George's agent at the time was Bill McMurdo. I knew Bill well because we had grown up together in Niddrie. I met George a couple of times through Bill. What struck me was that there was no side to him at all. He came across as really modest. In fact, I don't think that I heard him boast even once. He didn't need to, of course, because he had nothing to prove. His record spoke for itself.

I remember playing against George when he was at his peak. It was a Scotland versus Northern Ireland match at Hampden. I was playing at the back with Ronnie McKinnon of Rangers. Early in the game, George picked up the ball on the touchline around half way. He began to dribble across the pitch and looked like he was going nowhere. All of a sudden, he swivelled and chipped the ball towards goal. His effort only just cleared the bar. The crowd applauded and Ronnie and I looked at each other. Ronnie summed up how I was feeling when he said, 'Did you see that? It's going to be a long night.'

We managed to win 2–1 but George's class shone through. The same thing happened when he came to Hibs. At times he was magical and he was at his best when he came up against Rangers and Celtic. The top players are always big game players. I know from speaking to him that George enjoyed his time with Hibs. We certainly enjoyed having him.

Like Peter Marinello, George liked to wear his hair long. Another Hibs winger who favoured long hair was Willie Murray who played in the early seventies. Eddie Turnbull wasn't too impressed with Willie's hairstyle. He was even less impressed with his habit of carrying around his own hairdryer to use when he had showered after training. Men of Eddie's generation hadn't used hairdryers and he was always going on at Willie to get rid of his. Alex Ferguson is renowned for giving out the hairdryer. Eddie Turnbull was more concerned with taking it away.

When I was manager at Cowdenbeath, I signed Willie Murray on loan. Willie Ormond was Hibs manager at the time and he wasn't using Willie because he was planning to leave Hibs at the end of the season and immigrate to Australia. I asked Ormond if I could have Willie until then and he was good enough to agree to my request. One of Willie's first games was against Clyde. They were managed by Craig Brown and sitting top of the league. When they pulled up at Central Park in their team bus, they were all wearing club blazers and ties and really looked the business.

When the game started, Willie Murray tore them to ribbons. He had an unbelievable game and inspired us to a 5–1 win. In the boardroom after the game, our chairman, who was a housebuilder, was raving about Willie. He said, 'We've got to get him signed up on a long term contract.'

I told him that there was no chance of that happening since Willie was going Australia. The chairman tried again. He said to me, 'Tell him if he stays, I'll build him a house in Cowdenbeath.' When I put this offer to Willie, he didn't consider it a sufficient incentive to abandon his plans for emigration!

Another great winger was Mickey Weir, who signed for Hibs when I was manager. He was always a smashing wee player. If you were under pressure, you just gave the ball to Mickey and he was off and running. He could keep possession, make progress and allow you to move out as a team. Mickey had great ball control and was a better finisher than a lot of wingers.

Mickey was never short of opinions and he was always nagging at referees and linesmen. His best sustained spell of form was during the Skol League Cup winning run in 1991. Maybe that was because he was injury free at that time. Mickey was unlucky enough to pick up more than his fair share of knocks during his time at Hibs, which stopped him being an even better player than he was.

He was a top player though, and as I have already said, he was brilliant in 1991. His cross for Keith Wright's goal in the semi final against Rangers was perfect, as was his pass that Keith ran on to in the final to score the second goal. Mickey also earned the penalty that gave us the lead in that game. I'm not sure that there was too much contact on Mickey before he went down in the box but when I discuss it with him, he never shows the slightest trace of embarrassment.

Two of Alex Miller's more successful signings were Kevin McAllistair and Michael O'Neill. It was great to see Hibs playing with two wingers again and Kevin and Michael were two of the best. Kevin was as tricky as they come and was a real professional who looked after himself off the field. That's why he was able to keep playing for as long as he did. Michael had a lot of skill and a bit of a temper. He was bright on and off the pitch but did tend to get a bit fired up. He was certainly fired up on New Year's Day 1996. He scored Hibs' equaliser in the derby that day with a great near-post header. He then sprinted down the touchline in celebration. He was going so fast that the rest of the team couldn't catch him up. Michael's a manager back in Ireland now and with his intelligence and will to win, he could do well.

Jim Duffy signed Tony Rougier for Hibs from Raith Rovers. You just never knew what to expect from Tony. He had tons of talent. He would be a world beater one week and then the following week, he would be hopeless. Tony had the ability but he lacked the application. He left Hibs for Reading and later on a few other clubs in England signed him. A lot of managers obviously thought that they could get the best out of him on a consistent basis but I don't think that any of them really succeeded. Tony was just an easygoing big lad who played well when he was in the mood but didn't do so well when he wasn't.

He did Hibs one real favour though. It was Tony who recommended Russell Latapy to Alex McLeish. They had played together for Trinidad and Tobago and when Tony heard that Russell was between clubs, he gave Alex the word. Tony deserves our appreciation for doing that because Russell was a player of the highest class.

Alex McLeish signed Paul Hartley as a winger to replace Tony Rougier. We were in the First Division when Hartley joined. In one of his first games, he controlled a crossfield pass on the touchline with one touch and then kept the ball up as he moved down the wing. It looked great but it was a false dawn. Paul had his moments with Hibs but didn't really hit it off. You've got to give him credit for developing his career the way he did after he left Easter Road. I didn't expect him to reinvent himself as a midfield player at Hearts and go on to become a Scotland regular but he did exactly that. I could have seen him far enough during his time at Tynecastle because he kept coming back to haunt us.

Tony Mowbray brought Ivan Sproule from Northern Ireland for only £5,000. What a signing that was. Hibs fans loved Ivan.

Alan Rough, who played such a major part in keeping Hibs in the top league during my time as manager.

John Brownlie, a player of poise, pace and power who was equally brilliant at either end of the field. I always thought of him as a right winger in a right back's jersey.

The Brylcreem Boys: John Parke (right) meets his successor Joe Davis on the day he left Hibs to join Sunderland.

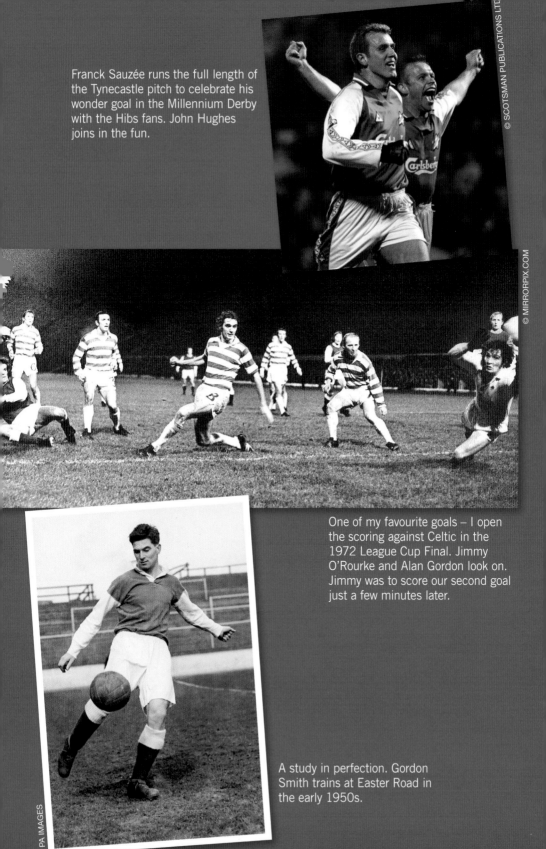

Franck Sauzée runs the full length of the Tynecastle pitch to celebrate his wonder goal in the Millennium Derby with the Hibs fans. John Hughes joins in the fun.

One of my favourite goals – I open the scoring against Celtic in the 1972 League Cup Final. Jimmy O'Rourke and Alan Gordon look on. Jimmy was to score our second goal just a few minutes later.

A study in perfection. Gordon Smith trains at Easter Road in the early 1950s.

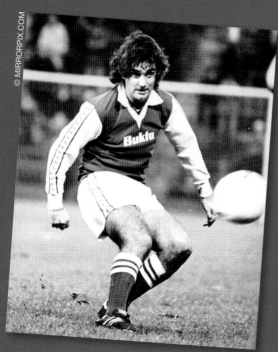

The genius that was George. George Best shows his class during his time with Hibs. The Irish legend enjoyed his time at Easter Road and we loved having him.

A happy team group with the 1964 Summer Cup. Man of the match Willie Hamilton, third from the left, gets his hands on the trophy.

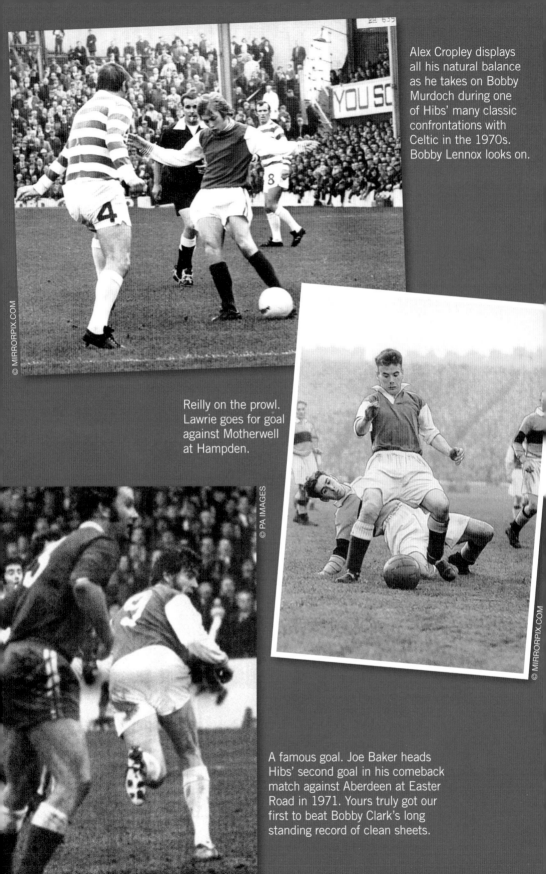

Alex Cropley displays all his natural balance as he takes on Bobby Murdoch during one of Hibs' many classic confrontations with Celtic in the 1970s. Bobby Lennox looks on.

Reilly on the prowl. Lawrie goes for goal against Motherwell at Hampden.

A famous goal. Joe Baker heads Hibs' second goal in his comeback match against Aberdeen at Easter Road in 1971. Yours truly got our first to beat Bobby Clark's long standing record of clean sheets.

© MIRRORPIX.COM

© PA IMAGES

© MIRRORPIX.COM

Jock Stein shows his man management skills as he makes time to encourage long term injury victims Jim Easton and George Gartshore during his early days in charge at Easter Road.

Tom McNiven works his healing magic on Chris Shevlane. Tom pioneered the use of technology to treat players' injuries. His 1960s heat lamp falls a little short of the facilities available these days in the club's new training complex at East Mains.

Rod Petrie, the man who has made Hibs financially sound, arrives at Hampden for a meeting with the SFA.

John Blackley calmly goes round Celtic's Dixie Deans before clearing the ball in the 1973 Drybrough Cup Final.

Bobby Johnstone, the player Joe Baker described as 'the best goal maker I ever played with'.

Alex Edwards, a player of huge talent and decidedly fiery temperament, shows off Hibs' new strip as the club blazes the trail by displaying a sponsor's name at the front of the players' jerseys.

The look says it all. Hibs have just lost 6-1 to Celtic in the 1972 Scottish Cup final. The expression on Jimmy O'Rourke's face sums up how all Hibs supporters and players felt on that dreadfully disappointing day. It also showed just how much Jimmy cared about our club.

John Collins celebrates a goal with Steve Archibald. They were two truly outstanding players.

Neil Martin looks the part during the pre-match warm up. He achieved the notable feat of scoring a century of goals on both sides of the border.

© SCOTSMAN PUBLICATIONS LTD

© MIRRORPIX.COM

Eric Stevenson shows that, unlike most left wingers, he can also use his right foot. Mind you, Eric's left was special. He conjured up magic with it on a regular basis.

Like Arthur Duncan, they liked his spirit and his obvious commitment to the cause. He had a bit of a personality as well and there was never a dull moment when Ivan was around. He could infuriate you but at his best he was electric. If you could have combined the skill of somebody like Alex Edwards with the pace and trickery of Ivan Sproule, you would have had a player worth twenty million pounds. Ivan got a few goals against the Old Firm and his hat trick at Ibrox will stay long in the memory.

I'm not sure why John Collins chose to move Ivan Sproule on. He had plenty to say for himself and maybe he had rubbed John up the wrong way at times. I don't think there was any harm in Ivan though. Hibs had sold Kevin Thomson, Scott Brown and Steven Whittaker so we didn't need the money. Quite a bit of the money we got for Ivan went towards signing Alan O'Brien. That's one signing that definitely didn't work out because O'Brien was never as successful or popular as Sproule.

It's been a pleasure to remember so many great Hibs wingers. When it comes to making my final choice though, it's not difficult to select my two wide men.

It has to be Gordon Smith on the right wing. You can't have a Hibernian Dream Team that doesn't include Gordon Smith. It's just unthinkable. I can still vividly remember that early game I played for Hibs against Dundee when they had Gordon on their side. Dundee had a really smart strip. It was dark blue with a white v-neck. It really suited Gordon and he looked magnificent in it. As I looked at him though, I couldn't help visualising him in the Hibs strip he had worn with such distinction for so many years. He looked even better in that. Gordon was genuinely world class and it's an honour to have him in my team.

I had to give serious consideration to Willie Ormond, Eric

Stevenson and Arthur Duncan for the left wing berth. They were all great players with different strengths. Willie's direct running and finishing earned him a great reputation at a time when Hibs had a wealth of forward talent. Eric had silky skills and an all round game. Arthur had pace and power and would run all day. The player I have chosen has all these attributes and more. He is, of course, the one and only Georgie Best.

If you picked an all time World team, you would automatically pick players like Gordon Banks, Carlos Alberto, Bobby Moore, Pelé and Maradona. All of these players have won the World Cup. George Best never even got the chance to play in the final stages of the World Cup. Yet he is right up there with the all time great players I have just mentioned. He would be an automatic selection in anyone's all time World team and he is definitely an automatic selection for my Hibernian Dream Team.

I would put George in the top three players I have seen in my lifetime. Maradona's my number one and Pelé comes next. I would have George in third place but there's not a lot in it. Given the exalted company that he's keeping that says a lot about George and how great he was.

What a team I'm building up here. I've got class in every area of my side but nowhere more than on the wings. Gordon Smith and George Best are a dream combination who will give the defenders who oppose them nothing but nightmares.

5

MIDFIELD MAESTROS

To win football matches, you have to control the middle of the park. If you let the other team dominate in that area, you will usually lose the game. You want your midfield players to be able to win possession and retain it. They also need to be able to create openings and score their fair share of goals. Doing all of these things at the highest level is not easy and only the very best players succeed in the centre of midfield. I am glad to say that over the years, Hibs have been blessed with midfield players of the highest quality.

When I was growing up, the Famous Five were ensuring that Hibs ruled Scottish football. In those days, midfield players were called wing halves or inside forwards. Hibs' inside forwards were truly magnificent players and they complemented each other perfectly. You couldn't get a better combination of graft and guile than Eddie Turnbull and Bobby Johnstone. Eddie was a tireless worker who was the Five's driving force. He powered the team's engine. Bobby was a silky player who made sure that the engine ran smoothly.

Don't get the impression that Eddie Turnbull was just a workhorse. He was a lot more than that. He could tackle, carry the ball, make passes and he got a lot of goals. Many of these goals came from the cannonball shots that Eddie was famous for. He fired these in from all distances and sometimes from the penalty spot. He once scored a hat trick of penalties against Celtic. I don't think any Hibs player will manage to replicate that achievement, since these days it is hard enough to win one penalty against the Old Firm, let alone three. One thing I will say about Eddie is that when he became Hibs manager, he never boasted about his playing career even though he had plenty to boast about. Some managers can't stop going on about their playing days. Eddie never did that.

Bobby Johnstone was a class act. He was a natural play-maker who could create a host of chances for his team mates. During Bobby's second spell at Hibs, the club scored goals galore. In one season, we scored over one hundred league goals. We scored eight against Third Lanark, ten against Partick Thistle and eleven against Airdrie. Bobby made many of these goals and Joe Baker scored a lot of them. These two were a deadly double act. Wee Bobby would make slide rule, defence-splitting passes and Joe would latch on to them and put the ball in the net. Johnstone got quite a few goals himself. He was a composed finisher and a player of great skill and artistry.

When Bobby came back to Hibs, he formed an excellent midfield partnership with John Baxter. When I first joined up at Easter Road, I used to really admire John. He was a great example to young players. He was always smartly turned out both on and off the field and trained conscientiously like the real professional that he was. I am not sure that he realised just how good an influence he was on the youngsters at the club at that time. He wasn't a bad player either. He got up and down the park with great energy and had a rocket shot in his left foot. In one game against Dundee, who were a top side at that time, Hibs went in 2–0 down at half time. In the second half, with Bobby Johnstone pulling the strings, Hibs surged into a 4–2 lead shooting down the slope. Joe Baker and John Baxter got two goals each.

Both of John's goals came from trademark bullet shots. Near the end, we got a penalty. Joe magnanimously stood back to allow John to take the spot kick and score his hat trick. Never a man for half measures, John took a long run up and blasted the ball as hard as he could. He failed to keep it down and the ball flew over the bar, over the crowd and into the road. I am not sure if John ever did manage a hat trick for Hibs but he certainly had his chance that day.

When William Harrower replaced Harry Swan as Hibs chairman, he gave the manager Walter Galbraith some money to spend. One of the first players Walter bought was Pat Quinn. Pat was a great wee player but he didn't half like a moan. He never stopped complaining during a game. Mind you he was usually giving you good advice. It was just that he delivered that advice in a torn faced manner. Pat could play though. He was a fine passer of the ball who played the game with style. He once scored a hat trick against Hearts at Tynecastle when we beat them 4–1. I think that he was the last Hibs player to achieve that feat until Mixu Paatelainen got three in the 6–2 win at Easter Road thirty-three years later.

When Pat later became a manager, he was really negative. Bertie Auld was the same. Bertie joined Hibs after he left Celtic and was still a cultured, crafty player with an educated left foot. As a manager, Bertie projected a flamboyant image with big talk and even bigger cigars. I think that was just a persona he cultivated for public consumption. Behind the scenes, he was friendly and helpful and a source of a lot of valuable advice.

When Bertie and Pat made up Hibs management team, the football would have put you to sleep. Hibs were really defensive under them. This was really surprising given that they had both been such talented and creative players themselves.

Maybe they were just making the best of the players that they had at their disposal. If this was the case, then they took things a wee bit too far.

Another player Walter Galbraith signed back in the sixties was Willie Hamilton. Willie's reputation went before him, of course. Wherever he had been, he had been successful on the field and irresponsible off it. When he came to Hibs, he wasn't in the best of physical shape but it was obvious that he could play. Willie was a character of contradictions. He was easy-going off the field and desperate to win on it. Although essentially good-natured, he could fly off the handle if he felt that other players weren't pulling their weight. He loathed the physical fitness side of training but would work with the ball all day if you asked him to.

Willie had talent to spare. He had amazing ball control and could dribble past players with ease. His passing was tremendous and he had surprising pace over ten to fifteen yards. Willie didn't look fast but he was deceptively quick. You only need speed over a short distance to leave your marker for dead and Willie had that. When you watched him in training and saw what he could do with a ball, it was an education for a young player.

Willie was less keen on fitness work. In those days our training sessions quite often started with lapping the track at Easter Road. Willie hated this. He would wait until he thought that Tom McNiven the physio wasn't watching and he would jump over the perimeter wall and hide behind it. After the rest of us had completed a few laps, Willie would rejoin us thinking that he had fooled McNiven. Tom knew fine what Willie was up to but he never let on. He knew that he would never change Willie so he didn't try to.

One man who was a good influence on Willie Hamilton though was Jock Stein. When Jock became manager, he recognised Willie's talent and decided to bring the best out of him. Willie admired Stein but he was scared of him, so during the Big Man's time he kept himself fitter than usual. Mind you, some days he still turned up looking the worse for wear. He always had a last cigarette before he came in to get changed because smoking was one of his vices as well. When training started, the perspiration was soon showing on the front of his top. We used to feel for him as he went through his paces. He never complained though, and by the end of his morning's work he would be as right as rain. I can still hear him now singing away in the shower after training. His favourite song was 'Twenty-Four Hours from Tulsa' and he used to give it big licks. Most footballers enjoyed a drink in those days but the majority would leave alcohol alone after a Wednesday. Willie had so much ability that he could misbehave right up until the end of the week and still perform on a Saturday afternoon.

The better the opposition, the better Willie played. When we met Real Madrid in 1964, Willie was really excited about the prospect of playing against Ferenc Puskás. The great Hungarian is one of the best players who ever lived but he was second best to Willie Hamilton in that game. To put it simply, Willie played him off the park.

We played Real on the Wednesday and went through to Glasgow to play Rangers on the following Saturday. Jim Baxter was the main man in Scottish football at that time and he was the master of all he surveyed at Ibrox. Jim was a magnificent player but Willie outclassed him that day. I don't think that it's an exaggeration to say that Willie ran riot in that game. He silenced the crowd and made Baxter look second best, which took a bit of doing. We won 4–2 and Willie Hamilton was unbelievably good.

Like Willie, Puskás and Baxter enjoyed the good life off the pitch. Maybe he should have invited them out for a drink after these two games to discuss his performances. He could have taken them to the Hibs club. That would have been some night!

Not long after these games, we played Hearts at Tynecastle in the New Year Derby. Hearts goalie Jim Cruickshank was one of the best. As the game neared the end, we were locked at 0–0. We got a free kick, which Pat Quinn took quickly. Pat sent Willie away and he reached the bye line to the left of Cruickshank's goal. Jim made his mind up that the angle was so tight that Willie would have to cross the ball, so he moved out in anticipation. He had forgotten that he was dealing with a genius. Willie swerved the ball into the top corner with the outside of his left foot to score one of the best goals I have ever seen and win the game for us.

As I said earlier, Willie liked to win. I remember one game that we had thrown away. In the dressing room afterwards, Willie was furious. He flung his boots against the wall and shouted, 'You're all a bunch of cowboys. I'm the only player at this club.' Nobody argued. We just all sat there thinking, 'Aye, you're probably right.'

Another time when Willie got fired up was during our close-season tour of America and Canada in 1965. One day we had a game in Ottowa. It was incredibly hot and none of us really fancied it too much. Except for Willie that is. He had heard that the man of the match would be awarded a silver salver and he was determined to win it. While the rest of us conserved our energy and ran to the touchline to take in some fluid, Willie played like a man possessed. He seemed oblivious to the extreme heat and covered miles. He scored seven goals and won the prized silver salver. Mind you, he couldn't have prized it that much because he bent it to make it fit into his luggage when we were coming home.

Willie could light up any game with his skill. He would produce a pass in a million or fire in a volleyed goal from nowhere. He left us with many memories. When you had seen Willie Hamilton playing football, you never forgot him. He was a lovely man. He was kind and generous to a fault and sadly, was in many ways his own worst enemy. It is well documented that Jock Stein rated Willie really highly and I agree with him. In terms of natural ability, he was right up there with the best of them. I would put him in the same bracket as the likes of George Best and Jim Baxter without a moment's hesitation.

I remember as a young player admiring Willie greatly. I went up to him one day and asked if he had any advice that he could share with me. He nodded his head, looked thoughtful for a moment and then said with total seriousness, 'Pat, son, never take lime in your lager and you'll no go far wrong in life.'

When Willie Hamilton was ripping Real Madrid and Rangers to shreds, Peter Cormack was making his way in the Hibs team. Stein introduced him as a teenager and initially played him on the right wing. Peter scored the first goal against Real and got two at Ibrox, which wasn't a bad four days work for a seventeen year old.

Peter also played as a striker for Hibs but he was at his best in midfield. A lot of players are versatile but Peter could play at the very highest level in three different positions, which takes a bit of doing. He was slim and wiry but brave. He was hard in the tackle and could be fiery. He had a real strong will to win.

Peter was a confident lad but he backed up his self-belief with his performances on the pitch. As his career developed, he wasn't afraid to tell his colleagues how to play during games but he usually kept his comments for the more experienced players and left the youngsters alone. Peter could be serious at times but he also had a mischievous sense of humour when the mood took him.

Peter was outstanding in the air. He got up miles and seemed to hang there. He put plenty of power into his heading of the ball as well. One of his best was against Napoli. He scored the goal that put us in front on aggregate. It was an amazing leap and an exceptional goal.

Peter would often play when he was carrying an injury and he had a never-say-die spirit. This stood him in good stead when he went down to England. The success he achieved with Liverpool showed just how good a player he was.

In Turnbull's Tornadoes, I was privileged to be part of a tremendously talented trio of midfield players. To my right was Alex Edwards and to my left was Alex Cropley. The two Alexes were very different types of players but they were both great to play with.

Edwards was a thinking player. His brain was never still for a second and he was always searching for openings. He had instant control and could pass the ball accurately over both long and short distances. He had the vision to see a pass and the ability to execute it. His skill level was such that if Eddie Turnbull wanted someone to demonstrate a difficult piece of technique in training, he always chose Mickey, as we called him. Edwards would never let his manager down. The funny thing was he used to have a moan about training all the time. He would ask why we were doing certain things or complain that he couldn't see the point of a particular exercise but he always did it and did it well.

In my opinion, Alex Edwards was the most talented player never to win a full cap for Scotland. If he had played for Rangers or Celtic, he would have finished his career with a host of caps. Part of Alex's problem, of course, was his fiery temperament. Lots of teams set out to rile him and they rarely failed. We would tell Alex before a game to keep calm and not allow his opponents to wind him up. He would agree to keep control but he hardly ever managed to. Referees didn't give him the protection he deserved and the SFA handed him some lengthy suspensions. Other players seemed to get away with a lot more than Mickey.

He was a crafty little fellow, Tricky Mickey. He was always up to something and you never knew what was coming next. His quick free kick that set me up for our first goal in the 1972 League Cup Final was a case in point. The pass he sent me away with for the second goal was also superb. He weighted it so perfectly that I didn't even have to break stride as I crossed it into the centre for Jimmy O'Rourke to head home.

One New Year derby match at Easter Road in the early seventies, we were taking care of Hearts comfortably. Alex was on top of his game and was really enjoying himself. The referee came up to me and said, 'Have a word with wee Edwards or I am going to have to send him off.' I looked over at Alex who was standing next to Jim Jefferies, the Hearts captain. He was serenading JJ with a little ditty based on Jingle Bells. Instead of singing, 'Oh what fun it is to ride on a one horse open sleigh,' Alex was singing, 'Oh what fun it is to beat the Hearts on New Year's Day.' Come to think of it, he was using a different word than 'beat'. Jefferies was apoplectic. His eyes were bulging out of his head and his veins were throbbing. I had to move Alex away before the referee took action but Alex, being Alex, couldn't resist turning round to give big Jim one last salvo before he ran back into position. I had to do my serious captain bit but it was all I could do to keep my face straight.

Alex Cropley approached the game in a more straight-forward fashion. He crunched into tackles, made exciting runs with the ball, matched Edwards in the art of the cross field pass and scored some spectacular goals. They say in football that a player is more likely to get injured if he pulls out of a tackle. That is true most of the time but sometimes in fact it is wiser not to commit yourself to a tackle. This was not a judgement that wee Cropley ever bothered to make. He always went in where it hurt. He usually came out with the ball but occasionally he got injured. Alex had a few bad injuries in his time and his courage contributed to that.

He was magnificent to watch in full flight. When Alex got a head of steam up, he was a great sight. He would run at defences with his long hair flowing and he was virtually impossible to stop. Defenders must have been terrified as he burst into their space. He always reminded me of a fox going into a chicken run. The defenders he faced would have known how the chickens felt.

Alex attempted a comeback with Hibs when he returned to Scotland after stints down south. I was manager then and I would have loved to have him in my team. Sadly the injuries he had picked up over the years stopped him from continuing his career.

Playing in midfield with Edwards and Cropley was a joy. They were so good that they made my life easy. No matter how hard or fast anyone fired a ball at them, they killed it instantly. They knew the right pass to make and always timed it just right. They never gave you man and ball at the same time.

Crop was a nippy sweetie but most great players are. The fact that teams of the calibre of Arsenal and Aston Villa signed him when he left Hibs shows how classy he was. He drives taxis for a living these days and I wouldn't want to get in his cab without the right money.

When John Brownlie moved to Newcastle, Ralph Callachan

came to Hibs as part of the deal. Ralph became a great servant to the club. His style was laid back and he could look lazy and lackadaisical but he was a player you underestimated at your peril. Ralph scored some good goals for Hibs and was a calming midfield presence during a period when the club was struggling. Ralph was such a well organised player that he could have played well in any outfield position.

I gave John Collins his debut for Hibs when he was just sixteen years old. He played in a friendly match against Manchester City and didn't look out of place. Jock Stein watched that game from the stand and told me afterwards, 'You've got a good one there.'

Although John was quiet, he never lacked self-confidence. When he was on the ground staff, he was friendly with a lad called Michael McManus. Michael's dad Jimmy had played with me at school at Holy Cross. Jimmy went on to play for Falkirk and Dundee United before moving to South Africa. His son came across to spend some time with us and he spoke with a strong South African twang. John, at that time, had a broad Galashiels accent. They used to talk away to each other non-stop and I could hardly understand a word they said. I remember telling them one day that trying to make out what they were saying was a bit like listening to the Flowerpot Men.

John was always dedicated. He was a neat little player who stayed composed and used the ball well. He scored a few goals but probably should have scored more. He was a great tackler. His tackling was so good that I am convinced that he could have played on as a left back for another couple of years if he had wanted to prolong his career. He obviously didn't feel the need as he had played successfully in Scotland, England and France and had carved out an excellent international career as well.

John did well financially. He fully earned everything he received as he committed himself totally to his profession. Plenty players these days seem to make a lot of money for very little effort. John Collins put in his absolute maximum and deserved any rewards that came his way.

Paul Kane often partnered John in Hibs' midfield in the eighties. Paul was a supporter on the pitch. He was, and is, a Hibs man through and through. Paul cares about our club and this showed every time he pulled on a Hibs jersey. Kano was never a showy player but he was consistent and scored some important goals. I think that we only realised how good he was when we no longer had him.

I always thought that Paul would make a good manager but he chose to go down the business route when he retired. He is very astute and I am sure that he will make a success of whatever he does. He is one of the main movers and shakers in the Hibs Former Players Association and does a great job there as well.

Alex Miller signed Pat McGinlay from Blackpool and it turned out to be a great move. Pat was a player who chased lost causes. He could run all day and he scored an awful lot of goals for a midfield player. Celtic recognised Pat's talent when they took him to Parkhead. Like all Hibs supporters, I was delighted when we brought him back to Easter Road. He was every bit as successful in his second spell as he had been in his first, which doesn't always happen with a player. In Hibs' promotion season of 1998–99, Pat played a key role. His experience was invaluable and he scored some vital goals.

I also thought that Pat timed his exit from Hibs well. He left when he was still a valuable player and the fans will only remember him as he was at his peak. Many players hang on too long and tarnish fans' memories of them by doing this. Pat knew when it was time to move on.

Pat played in the 1991 Skol Cup winning team, of course, and scored typical goals in a couple of the early rounds of the competition. Murdo McLeod captained that team and proved to be a shrewd acquisition on Alex Miller's part. By the time he joined Hibs, Murdo wasn't able to get into the kind of positions that he used to take up regularly for Celtic. This meant that he no longer scored as many spectacular goals. His experience was crucial though. He was a tough wee player and could look after himself and those around him. Murdo was a major influence for the good both on and off the park during his time with Hibs. I think he enjoyed his spell at Easter Road and I suspect he still retains a soft spot for our club. Come to think of it, why wouldn't he?

Murdo hasn't been too well of late and I am sure that all Hibees wish him a speedy return to full health.

When Jim Duffy took over as Hibs manager, he seemed to be trying to get into the Guinness Book of Records by signing a record number of players. Sadly, quite a number of his signings have to be classed as failures. He got some right though. I think most fans would consider that Jim's best move was bringing in Chic Charnley.

James Charnley, to give him his proper name, was a maverick, a cheeky chappie and a top class football player. With the talent he had, Chic should have played at the highest level for a very long time. Unfortunately, discipline was never his strong point and that held him back.

A lot of people think that his real name is Charles, which is where the nickname 'Chic' comes from. Not so; as a boy he sold frozen chickens round the estate he lived in. The locals nicknamed him 'Chic' and the name stuck.

When he was at Hibs, the fans really took to him. It was clear that he loved playing football and his enthusiasm for the game was infectious. He had huge ability, which he proved when he scored from the halfway line against Alloa. Pelé tried to score from halfway and narrowly missed in the 1970 World Cup Finals. David Beckham eventually managed it in England but Chic did it first in Scotland. Not long after Chic did it, Pat McGinlay managed to repeat the feat, so Hibs probably still hold the record for scoring fifty yard goals.

When Chic played for Celtic as a guest in a testimonial match against Manchester United, the story goes that he had the nerve to nutmeg the great Eric Cantona. I don't know what Eric made of this piece of skill but I am sure that Chic was absolutely delighted.

Before Alex McLeish converted Franck Sauzée into a sweeper, Hibs had their best midfield trio since Mickey, Crop and I used to team up for Eddie Turnbull. Franck, John O'Neil and Russell Latapy were a formidable combination. They also received valuable support from the underrated but highly effective powerhouse that was Matty Jack.

Franck's debut for Hibs was in a vital promotion battle with Falkirk at Brockville. It was a dreich day and a hostile atmosphere. Franck hadn't played for a few weeks and had a quiet game. His class shone through though and he made the winning goal for Derek Collins with a neat backheel.

Russell revolutionised Hibs. He was that good. He used to occupy a position ahead of the midfield and behind the strikers. This made it really hard for defenders to pick him up. He could run with the ball, beat players for fun and score brilliant goals. To the delight of Hibs supporters and the dismay of Hearts fans, he always seemed to reserve his best displays for derby matches. His goal in the 6–2 match was a thing of beauty. Russell was alleged to be a bit of a playboy off the field but he managed to keep playing until he was nearly forty. Maybe he was blessed with a lot of natural fitness. Dean Martin used to say that if he had got up to half the things that the tabloid newspapers claimed he had, he would have been dead long ago. It could be that reports of Russell's off field activities were exaggerated as well. One thing's for sure, he was a top player and his style of play fitted perfectly into the Hibs tradition.

The Hibs fans loved Russell. Even though he left us to sign for Rangers, he always got a great reception when he came back to Easter Road in his Falkirk days. Given that our supporters don't forgive and forget easily, the level of welcome accorded to Russell speaks volumes about the kind of player he was.

John O'Neil did a lot of solid work that freed up Franck and Russell to weave their magic. John was an excellent player for Hibs and the importance of his contribution to Alex McLeish's team shouldn't be overlooked.

Tony Mowbray inherited a couple of cracking young midfield players in Scott Brown and Kevin Thomson. Brown is great at running with the ball and is as hard as nails. He is an expert at upsetting his opponents. When your opponents lose their composure, they don't perform well and Scott has made an art of rubbing players up the wrong way. He played a major role in the club winning the 2007 CIS League Cup and although we all knew that he would move eventually, he stayed with us long enough to bring home that trophy. He gave one hundred per cent effort for Hibs right up to the end when he scored a header against Celtic in his last game at Easter Road. The club received an excellent fee for Scott and he left with the fans' best wishes.

That can't really be said about Kevin Thomson. Before his first cruciate ligament injury, he was a hard tackling, ball carrying midfielder who linked the play really well. I don't think he's been quite as good since. Kevin left Hibs under a bit of a cloud as a lot of fans thought that he didn't show the club proper respect when he made it obvious that he was keen to leave.

Tony Mowbray inherited Brown and Thomson but he was personally responsible for bringing Guillaume Beuzelin to Easter Road. When Beuzelin first arrived he was an elegant play-maker who complemented the two young players to either side of him perfectly. Sadly, his time at Hibs was blighted by injury. He had the option of signing a new contract but chose to move to Coventry. He might be regretting that now after his release by the Midlands club. Too many players move on from Hibs and then, when it's too late, realise just how good a club they've left behind. I suspect Beuzelin is now one of these players.

Another Tony Mowbray signing was Merouane Zemmama. The little Moroccan is a really talented player. His control is excellent and he can turn defenders inside out with his trickery. Unfortunately, he is prone to drift out of the game. He must keep himself involved more. When the ball doesn't come his way, he has to go looking for it. Equally, his team mates have to make sure that they find him with the ball on a regular basis. Zouma is a match winner and it makes sense to supply a player like him with the ball as often as possible. In my opinion though, Zemmama doesn't deliver consistently enough. On his good days, he is exceptional but for a player of his ability, his good days are far too few and far between.

Liam Miller was one of John Hughes' first signings. His pedigree is impressive. You don't play for Celtic and Manchester United unless you have something to offer. What Miller offers is an ability to take the ball and move it on accurately. He does the simple things well and makes the right choices most of the time. This sounds easy and supporters watching a player like Miller might think to themselves, 'I could do that,' but it's not nearly as simple as it looks. Neil Lennon and Paul Lambert were two other players who perfected the art of the simple. If it really was easy, everyone would do it.

I thought that my final choice of two central midfield players would be really tough but in fact I have made my decision quickly and with complete certainty. I am going for Willie Hamilton and Alex Cropley.

Willie was like a shooting star crossing the sky. He was there for far too short a time but his impact has stayed with us. Jock Stein thought he was one of the best and he didn't get too many things wrong in his time in football. I can honestly say that in all my years supporting, playing for and managing Hibs, I have never seen a more naturally talented player in the green and white than Willie when he was on song.

Alex was the ideal left sided midfielder. He was a defender, a creator and a scorer all in one player. His frame was slight but his heart was huge. He was bursting with ability and I am very happy to have such a great player in my midfield.

When working people go to the football on a Saturday, they are looking for a magical moment from a great player to transform their week. Both Willie and Alex provided these moments on a regular basis. You've witnessed something special and when you go home and try to describe it, you just can't do it justice. You had to be there to fully appreciate it. When you're watching a match and a piece of footballing greatness occurs, you never forget it. You might forget the score or the scorers but you always remember the piece of breathtaking skill that you've had the privilege to watch. Only special players give us these kinds of memories. Willie Hamilton and Alex Cropley were two very special players and they will be in centre midfield in my Hibernian Dream Team.

6

STRIKING SUPERSTARS

The opposition penalty area is the business end of the pitch. That's where football's glamour boys do their stuff. A successful striker is guaranteed the adulation of the crowd and more than a fair share of the post match headlines. For those reasons, many players aspire to the striking position.

It's only when you try playing up front that you realise how difficult it actually is. You are marked closely by defenders, you have to constantly make runs to lose these defenders, you require the ability to hold the ball up under pressure and the skill to bring your team mates into play and most of all you have to be able to be in the right place at the right time and take a chance or indeed a half chance when it presents itself.

Top strikers then deserve the plaudits which come their way. At their best they can supply the goals which win matches and trophies. That is why they are always in demand and why football clubs are prepared to pay so much for their services.

Hibs have been incredibly blessed in the striking department. As I approached my eighth birthday, Hibs were winning the old First Division Championship for the third time in five years. Their centre forward was a veritable goal machine called Lawrie Reilly. I used to listen to my dad and granddad talking about Lawrie and it was clear from the way they spoke that they held him in the highest regard. No wonder that was the case. Lawrie never stopped scoring goals for Hibs and Scotland. He was Scotland's all time top scorer for a very long time until he was eventually overtaken by Denis Law and Kenny Dalglish. Both of these all time great Scottish strikers had to play more games for their country than Lawrie to pass his total. Even when they retired, their goals per game averages were inferior to 'Last Minute Lawrie'. Lawrie earned his nickname for his ability to snatch games out of the fire by scoring vital, late goals most notably, of course, against England at Wembley. In all, Lawrie scored five times at the famous ground in London and that of course was in the days when the Scotland versus England fixture was the highlight of the footballing calendar. Lawrie's dad kept scrapbooks detailing his career and he was able to use the information in the books to work out that his son had scored no fewer than nineteen last minute goals for club and country.

These days, Lawrie and I are good friends. We have played golf together and we regularly join forces to watch Hibs play. On the golf course Lawrie is fiercely competitive. In the stand supporting his beloved Hibs, he is fully engrossed in every game, sets high standards for the players in green and white jerseys and never accepts second best. I am sure that these characteristics which he still displays in his eighties today are what made him the player he was. He was desperate to win and used all his pace and prowess to ensure that he did.

Players like Lawrie Reilly usually come along once in a lifetime. Brazil have never found the second Pelé, Portugal are still seeking the next Eusebio and Holland continue to await the next Johan Cruyff. Amazingly, Lawrie Reilly's successor was another world class centre forward, and I don't use the term lightly, in Joe Baker.

As a young boy playing football, Joe Baker was my hero. He was an unbelievable player. The former Evening News football reporter Stewart Brown summed Joe up perfectly when he described him as 'a one man goal machine with two good feet, great pace and an excellent ability in the air – a combination rarely seen in modern football'.

When I was fourteen or fifteen years old, I used to spend my school summer holidays training with Hibs. Joe was there at that time and I think it's fair to say that I was in awe of him. The first thing that struck you was that he had style. He was a handsome man, always smartly dressed and usually driving a flashy car. He was no fancy Dan though. He always had time for us youngsters. Some of the older players, most of them with much less ability than Joe, could be hard on the emerging talent. They were of the old school and it was a hard school. They thought regularly putting us in our place would help to make us better footballers in the long run. Joe took a different approach. He remembered all our names and was always ready with a bit of praise or a piece of advice for me. These words coming from somebody whom I idolised meant an awful lot to me.

By the time I had broken into Hibs' first team, Joe had left the club. As we all know, he went on to play at the very highest level for Torino, Arsenal and Nottingham Forest. When Joe was at Forest they came very close to winning the League title. They met Hibs in a pre-season friendly at Easter Road prior to the start of the 1966–67 season. I couldn't wait to play against Joe and I was particularly intrigued to see how he would get on against our centre half John McNamee. Big John was a walking rock and very few centre forwards got the better of him. He was particularly strong in the air and stood well over six feet tall. Joe couldn't have been more than five feet nine if he was even that. Early in the game, the Notts Forest winger crossed the ball into the Hibs box. Joe got in front of McNamee and bulleted the ball into the net with his head. It was a great goal and the thing which struck me most was that Joe was at the height of his jump as Big John was coming down from his. It was pure timing and pure class. The game finished 2–2 and needless to say Joe scored both the Forest goals.

One of the games Joe is best remembered for is the Scottish Cup tie against Hearts in 1958. Joe was only seventeen at the time and Hearts were on their way to winning the League Championship. Hibs were major underdogs but managed to win 4–3 with the teenage terror at centre forward scoring all four goals. I wasn't at that match but I remember my dad and granddad discussing it afterwards. My granddad was saying that all the radio and television pundits had been saying that they didn't know who this young striker was. My dad chipped in: 'Aye, well they know who he is now!'

I was as excited as any supporter when I heard that Joe Baker was coming back to Hibs in 1971. We were playing Aberdeen at Easter Road. Bobby Clark the Aberdeen and Scotland goalkeeper hadn't conceded a goal for 1093 minutes – a record only recently beaten by Manchester United goalkeeper Edwin Van De Saar – and the Dons had won fifteen matches in succession. What an atmosphere there was inside Easter Road that day. A tremendous crowd turned up to welcome Joe back. He led the team out as captain and it was clear that he hadn't lost his sense of style. He wore a pair of white boots and sported a trendy set of sideburns.

It was his play which caught the eye though. He scored Hibs' second goal with a diving header and had another goal disallowed as we won 2–1 to bring Aberdeen's long run to an end.

I am pleased to say that I scored the first goal and spoiled Bobby Clark's record for keeping his goal intact. Later, Bobby and I played together for Scotland against Portugal and I managed to put an own goal past him. 'You'll be going for your hat trick now,' he said, referring of course to the goal which broke his record.

Joe must have been over thirty when he came back to Hibs but he could still play. We used to do sprint challenges in training and over twenty or thirty yards, he was electric. Jimmy O'Rourke and I watched him in amazement and I remember Jimmy saying, 'If he's like that now what must he have been like when he was nineteen or twenty?' One thing is for sure, when Joe got in front of a defender there was absolutely no chance of him being caught.

One last thought on Joe's sense of style. He always turned up looking extremely debonair and he had a real natty dress sense. One day Joe turned up for a match wearing a fawn suit and burgundy shirt and tie. The handkerchief in his top suit pocket matched his shirt perfectly. Jimmy and I wondered how he had managed to match his outfit up so expertly. We found out when he took off his trousers – there was a hole in the shape of a handkerchief cut out of his shirt tail!

Joe's premature passing was a great loss to the whole Hibs community. He and I both spoke at the rally organised by 'Hands off Hibs' to keep Hibs in existence when the club was under threat from Wallace Mercer's hostile takeover bid. It was obvious that day just how much Joe loved our club as he spoke about 'The Hibernian Family' and knelt to kiss the turf. It was clear too from the reception he received that the fans still loved him. Joe's bubbly presence round Easter Road on match days is sadly missed since he left us.

Joe was succeeded as Hibs centre forward by his brother Gerry. I played with Gerry at the beginning of my Hibs career. He was an excellent player who possessed even more speed than his brother, or so Gerry would have claimed anyway. I wasn't the least bit surprised when his daughter Lorraine became an Olympic runner. Pace was definitely in the Baker genes. I remember I played in a League Cup semi final against Morton with Gerry. Before the game he said to me, 'Make sure you just do it as it happens.' He meant that I should guard against going on the field with preconceived notions. Just because something had worked in a previous match, didn't mean that it would succeed every time. I had to be ready to respond to situations as they arose in games and to use my wits and skills to adapt to them. It was sound advice and I carried it through my career.

Inevitably Gerry had to put up with adverse comparisons with his younger brother during his time with Hibs. He must have been sick of hearing the crowd tell him that 'he would never be as good as Joe'. Gerry was the first to acknowledge that and was clearly very proud of his superstar sibling. Make no mistake though, Gerry could play. You don't score ten goals in one match as Gerry did in a Scottish Cup tie against Glasgow University without having a fair amount of ability.

The last time I bumped into Gerry, he looked years younger than his age and it was good to catch up with someone who was a nice man and an excellent centre forward.

When Walter Galbraith took over as Hibs manager, he demonstrated a really good eye for a player. He brought in class players like John Parke, Pat Quinn, Willie Hamilton and Neil Martin. He paid Queen of the South only £7000 for Martin which was a real bargain.

Neilly was a right good player. He was a great header of the ball, could finish with either foot and wasn't slow either. He had a real presence on the park. Neilly wasn't afraid of any defender but there were plenty centre halves who were wary of him. As well as having a lot of ability, he was brave and really determined. He had some great games for us but I think his best performance was when he scored a hat trick against Celtic at Parkhead. It was not long after Jock Stein had left us to go back to Celtic and we travelled through to Glasgow with a point to prove. Prove it we did because by half time we were 4–0 up and big Neilly had scored three of them. Celtic pulled back two goals in the second half but we walked away thinking that we had let our old boss know that there was still plenty talent at Easter Road. Neilly never made any secret of his desire to move to England at some stage and when he left for Sunderland, Hibs got a good fee in return. The big man did well down south too, scoring a lot of goals for Sunderland, Nottingham Forest and Coventry.

Colin Stein came to Hibs as a left back but Bob Shankly, who was manager by then, turned him into a centre forward. It turned out to be an inspired move. Colin was gangly, quick and strong. He was a really wholehearted player who chased lost causes all the time. He was hugely competitive and a natural games player. When he took up golf, he very quickly got to grips with the game and reached a good standard. I think he also reached a good level in bowls when he retired from football.

He was an excellent footballer though and scored a lot of good goals for Hibs. One of his best was against Napoli and he also scored against Leeds United in the Fairs Cup. The fans loved Stein until he announced that he wanted a transfer and that the team he wanted to play for was Rangers. We players knew that Colin was a Rangers supporter but it came as a surprise to the supporters. He got his move and did really well at Ibrox but its fair to say that his popularity among the Easter Road faithful declined dramatically. During his time at Ibrox, Colin Stein scored five goals in a World Cup game for Scotland against Cyprus and scored one of the goals when Rangers won the European Cup Winners' Cup. He was a more than useful player.

Hibs got £100,000 from Rangers for Colin Stein and used less than £20,000 of it to buy Joe McBride. What a great bit of business that was. Joe was born to score goals. If he was one on one with the goalkeeper, you could put your mortgage on him to score. He scored one of the best Hibs goals I ever saw against Celtic when we beat them 2–0 at Easter Road. Joe got both goals but the swivelling volley which he produced for one of them showed just how good a striker he was.

I first encountered Joe on the day I made my first team debut for Hibs. He was playing for Motherwell against us at Fir Park. I mentioned earlier that Walter Galbraith was an excellent judge of a player.

He was but like all of us he wasn't infallible. Before the game at Motherwell that day, Walter went through the opposition listing their strengths and weaknesses. When he came to Joe McBride, he simply said 'deadly on the ground, not so good in the air'.

Early in the game, Joe bulleted a header into our net. At half time, one of our players said to Galbraith, 'Boss, I thought you said that McBride couldn't head the ball.' Our unflappable manager simply replied, 'None of us is right all the time son.' We lost 4–3 that day but I did manage to get a goal. It was also Willie Toner's last game for Hibs.

One of McBride's best games for Hibs was in Europe against Hamburg. We had lost 1–0 in Germany and won 2–1 at Easter Road. Uwe Seeler scored their goal and it put us out on the away goals rule. It was a complete travesty because we played really well that night. Joe Davis missed a penalty which wasn't like him but Joe McBride scored two goals. He also had two goals chalked off wrongly for offside. Maybe part of the referee's problem was that the green jersey worn by the Hamburg goalkeeper clashed with our strip. The referee hadn't even noticed this and it probably confused him when he was making his offside decisions. Joe's son also played for Hibs. He was a left winger and he wasn't a bad player either.

When Eddie Turnbull took over as manager, he made Alan Gordon one of his first signings. I had always admired Alan when he played for Hearts. He was an intelligent man and a thoughtful footballer. One goal that demonstrated this was against Partick Thistle at Firhill. Joe Harper had joined us by then and he had the ball out on the left touchline. Alan Gordon was being tightly marked and ran to the back post. The defender went with him but Alan suddenly changed direction and sprinted to the near post. Harper picked him out with a perfect cross and Alan scored with the defender nowhere in sight. I watched all this from the halfway line and what impressed me was the footballing intelligence of both players. They both instinctively saw the scoring move but the defender didn't. Alan was no bruiser but he was brave and held the ball up really well. He was good at bringing other players into the game as well.

Alan was also a composed and consistent finisher and a regular goal scorer. He came very close to winning the Golden Boot for Europe's top scorer during his time with Hibs. He was an expert header of the ball and this aerial prowess enabled him to score goals himself and create goals for others. I really liked Alan both as a man and a player and his recent passing was a source of great sadness to me.

Alan's strike partner, of course, was my pal Jimmy O'Rourke. Jimmy and I went to school together and believe you me Jimmy was some schoolboy footballer. He scored goals for our school, Holy Cross, Edinburgh Schools and Scotland Schools. He played in the same Scotland Schoolboy team as Peter Lorimer the great Leeds United player.

Jimmy made his debut for Hibs when he was just over sixteen and got off to a great start until he got a bad injury at Tannadice. He came back well though and developed his skills playing in different positions. By the time he teamed up with Alan Gordon, he was at the height of his game. He was a really bright player – bright in his head and bright in the way he approached the game. He never stopped running and the fans loved him. He was one of their own of course – a Hibee through and through.

He was a much better all round player than people gave him credit for. His decoy runs created the space for Alex Edwards and Alex Cropley to make their defence splitting passes in Eddie Turnbull's great team. He was great with dead balls as well.

I remember one game against Aberdeen when Jimmy and I were lined up over a free kick on the edge of the box. Jimmy said, 'I'm looking right at the stanchion in the corner of the net.'

'Well you take it and put it there,' I said. He did exactly that, planting a perfect shot in the exact spot that he had pinpointed. After that, I left all the free kicks to Jimmy. I remember another one he scored against Falkirk. His cousin Denis Devlin was in goal for Falkirk. Jimmy knocked a free kick past Denis and he was delighted. When the referee ordered a retake, Jimmy just put the ball down and repeated the exercise, placing the ball in the net once more. He was even more delighted after that.

When we beat big Stein's Celtic 2–1 to win the League Cup in 1972, Jimmy and I scored the goals and his was a beauty. Mind you mine wasn't too bad either. For Jimmy's goal, Alex Edwards sent me away with a great pass and I chipped the ball in to the near post where Jimmy had made a great run. He flew through the air and bulleted the ball past Evan Williams with his head.

We played really well in that final and were comfortable at 2–0 until Kenny Dalglish pulled one back for Celtic with eight minutes to go. It was a long eight minutes, I can tell you, but we held out. At that time, teams were banned from doing a lap of honour with the cup after a cup final victory. Knowing this, Jimmy suggested that we go to our fans when the final whistle blew and I agreed. It was an unforgettable experience for both the players and the brilliant support we had that day. We wouldn't have been able to go to the crowd after the presentation of the cup so Jimmy's quick thinking made a great moment possible. Jimmy was a quick thinker during games as well and Eddie Turnbull left him out of the Hibs team and sold him to St Johnstone when he still had an awful lot to offer. I've never been able to understand why Eddie did that.

Leaving aside his ability, and he had plenty of that, Jimmy was a great presence in the dressing room. He was always cheery and upbeat and had a wicked sense of humour. During one of our summer trips to North America, we were taken on a coach trip to see the infamous San Quentin State Prison. There was no sign of Johnny Cash the day we were there but when we were sitting outside looking at the building, a police van drew up. A number of prisoners, all dressed in orange boiler suits and all flanked by two warders, were brought out of the van and taken into the prison. Jimmy was staring intently at the prisoners as they were led past us. Bob Shankly was the manager and he said, 'What is it that you're looking at Jimmy?'

Jimmy replied, 'I was just making sure that there was naebody there that I knew from Clermiston.'

Joe Harper's signing signalled the beginning of the end for Jimmy. We paid too much for Joe and we didn't need him as Alan and Jimmy were scoring goals for fun. When it ain't broke, don't fix it.

Joe was a top striker though. He scored some great goals for us and none was better than his winner in the 1974 League

Cup semi final against Falkirk at Tynecastle. Joe curled the ball into the top corner of the net from the left edge of the box. It was a beauty. We went on to lose 6–3 in the final but wee Joe helped himself to a hat trick. He scored a tremendous long-range goal for us in a 1–0 derby win at Easter Road and yet another excellent winner against Liverpool at Easter Road.

Joe scored two goals at Parkhead in a game against Celtic that we were leading 2–0 with seven minutes to go. It started to get a bit foggy and the referee Bobby Davidson decided to abandon the game. Can you imagine him having done this if the score had been in Celtic's favour? He would never have dared but he did it to us. We all felt a huge sense of injustice. Our outrage was even stronger when the SFA decided that the whole game should be replayed. I think that if Sir Bob Kelly had still been Celtic chairman, he would have insisted on the points being awarded to Hibs. His boardroom succes-sors made no such suggestion and we had to do it all again. We drew the replayed match 1–1, which would normally have been a decent result. This time though, it felt like a defeat.

Just like now, you didn't get much in the way of breaks from referees when you went to Ibrox or Parkhead. Crowd pressure plays a big part in it. It can't be easy to stop your-self pointing to the spot when sixty thousand fans are screaming for a penalty. It's not just the influence of the crowd though; sometimes referees give decisions in favour of the Old Firm when nobody has even appealed for them. When he retired, one referee stood up at a football dinner and boasted that throughout his long career, Rangers had never lost a game in which he had been in charge.

It's easy for players to blame the officials though. Sometimes we have good reason, other times less so. We were all guilty of pointing the finger at the ref when responsibility really lay closer to home in terms of our own performance.

Joe Harper was never fully accepted by the Hibs fans probably because he had replaced Jimmy O'Rourke and he made it clear in his recent autobiography that he hadn't really wanted to join Hibs in the first place. Tom Hart simply made him too good an offer to refuse. I am sure that Joe was happy when he left Hibs to return to Aberdeen. There is no doubt though that he was a player of the highest class.

Ally McLeod was Hibs' next quality striker after Joe Harper moved on. I really liked Ally. He was sharp as a tack both on and off the field – a clever lad with a wicked sense of humour. He had a reputation for being lazy but Ally would argue that there was no point in wasting energy.

Ally didn't believe in work rate for work rate's sake but he could change gear when he had to. He was an easygoing, confident lad but he trained hard. He was a composed finisher who used to pass the ball into the net. I remember one game against Dundee at Easter Road when Ally plucked a long cross field pass from Alex Edwards out of the air with one touch. He then effortlessly stroked the ball into the corner of the net past the goalkeeper. In scoring that goal, he made the very difficult look ridiculously simple but that was Ally. He scored one short of a hundred goals for Hibs and as a player, he was easy on the eye. He was always a favourite of mine.

When John Blackley succeeded me as manager at Easter Road, he was given some money to spend. One of John's first signings was Gordon Durie from East Fife. A lot of clubs had looked at Durie but hadn't signed him which surprised me. Well, John took the plunge and was rewarded for doing so. Durie was fast and strong and a good striker. I liked his partnership with Stevie Cowan. They brought the best out in each other and scored goals galore especially during the run to the League Cup Final in 1985.

Like many before him and since of course, Durie didn't

overstay his welcome at Easter Road. He had good moves to Chelsea, Tottenham and Rangers before signing for Hearts. When he came back to his old stamping ground at Easter Road wearing maroon, he was on the wrong end of a 6–2 hammering in October 2000 so that certainly wasn't a case of many happy returns.

Another terrific striker was Steve Archibald who came to Hibs from Barcelona towards the end of the 1980s. I first saw Stevie when he was playing for Clyde in a Glasgow Cup tie. I was in Celtic's colours that day and it was obvious that the youngster in the opposition ranks was a bit special. I worked with Stevie when I was Alex Ferguson's assistant at Aberdeen. I liked him. He had a spark about him. He would argue his corner and didn't hold back on expressing his views. He never bore grudges afterwards though no matter how heated the discussion had been. He was a really good footballer who could have played in any outfield position and done well. His best goal for Hibs was against Hearts at Tynecastle in early 1989. Paul Kane had given Hibs the lead but Gordon Rae had been sent off. Hibs' ten men were only just holding on to their lead when Kano sent Stevie away. He was left of centre as he bore down on the Hearts goal. Dave McPherson was pursuing him and catching him with every stride. Henry Smith was advancing from his goal to narrow the angle. At the split second, big Davie thought he had caught him up and Henry thought that he was in position to block his shot, Stevie hit the ball and struck it sweetly into the corner of the net. It was a masterpiece of calculated timing and a finish of the highest quality. His celebration after scoring was pretty good as well.

When Keith Wright joined Hibs in 1991, I was pleased to see him come home to the club he supported. He made the perfect start by scoring in every game in the Skol League Cup run that year and, of course, he got the second goal in the final when wee Mickey Weir put him through with a great pass. Keith was a great player for the Hibs. He scored a lot of goals and always made himself available for the ball. As a defender or a midfield player, it is great to have a centre forward who gives you an out ball. Keith was an expert at that. He would always show himself, take the ball and hold it till his defence got out.

Keith formed a great partnership with Darren Jackson. Darren was a late developer. I think he played his best football with Hibs. He upset his opponents and scored some really great goals. Darren was the kind of player I would always have in my side. He had a great attitude, worked really hard and always put the opposition on the back foot.

When Alex McLeish brought in Mixu Paatelainen, a lot of people raised their eyebrows and thought that Mixu's best was behind him. Nobody would have blamed him if he had allowed his career to wind down a bit when he came to Easter Road. Nothing could have been further from the truth. He gave his all for Hibs and was a much underrated member of McLeish's successful team. He also scored a hat trick against the Hearts of course and that's something which nobody will ever be able to take away from him.

Franck Sauzée was the first to give Garry O'Connor his opportunity and I liked Garry from the minute I saw him play. He was an exciting young striker and he clearly listened to his coaches because there was perceptible improvement in all aspects of his game from season to season. By the time he left, he wasn't just chasing about, he was leading the line. It was a big loss to the club when he went to Russia.

Derek Riordan came through at the same time as Garry. I think that Derek's got the lot. He has so much natural talent. He can score both simple and spectacular goals as well as being able to make the killer pass.

I don't think Derek has fulfilled his potential yet. Great players create a legacy by leaving a range of exceptional performances in the supporters' minds. Derek's capable of doing that but he hasn't done it yet. All he's done so far is score a lot of goals, which is not to be taken lightly, but he is capable of contributing more to the team's general game since he's not short of all round ability. He needs to perform for whole games and not just drift in and out of a match as he does at the moment. It would be nice to see him smile a bit more too. The fans love Derek, and rightly so, but as often as not his face is tripping him when he's on the park. To me, there is no better footballing experience than playing for the Hibs. Derek should lighten up and enjoy it more.

Steven Fletcher gave Hibs five good seasons and they got good money for him when he left so he owes us nothing. He is a talented lad who has notched some first class goals. Maybe too much was expected of him at Hibs or maybe he just had too much to do but I think he sometimes suffered from being our only likely scorer. He could be isolated up front and this made it easier for defences to snuff him out.

Anthony Stokes is the latest in the long line of top quality Hibs strikers and he has a lot to offer. John Hughes has consistently selected him and Stokes has gained confidence from this. He is very good at getting into scoring positions but misses as many chances as he puts away. He does get some great goals though. His strike at Ibrox not long after he signed for Hibs was right out of the top drawer.

When Stokes was named as Young Player of the Month, he spoke about being much better prepared to play in the English Premier League than he had been when he joined Sunderland and failed during his first spell in the top league down south. I think he's deluding himself a little. To me, the SPL is Stokes' correct level and he should settle for excelling in it. You shouldn't try to kid yourself. Accept what you are and make the best of what you have.

I really like both Stokes and Riordan as players but one thing struck me forcibly when I was watching Manchester City play Manchester United in the Carling Cup semi final recently. Carlos Tevez and Wayne Rooney both played exceptionally well, as you would expect as they are world class strikers. What caught my eye though was their work rate. It was phenomenal. They just never stopped.

Derek and Stokesy don't put in anything like that level of effort. Why not? They're young men and should be bursting with fitness. Surely what's good enough for Tevez and Rooney is good enough for Riordan and Stokes.

I'm sure you'll agree that the gallery of goal scoring galacticos which I've looked at is very impressive indeed. Now I have to make my final choice. In making that choice, I have focused mainly on goal scoring ability because, to me, that's what being a striker is all about. I haven't looked at such modern concepts as 'defending from the front'. I don't think centre forwards should be chasing to and fro across the opposition back line. They should be conserving their energy for putting the ball in the net.

Mind you asking forwards to do a wee bit defending is nothing new. I remember a game against Raith Rovers at Kirkcaldy when Jock Stein was in charge. Before the game, Jock warned us that Davie Sneddon, their inside forward, would run the game if we let him. He told us to hit him hard early on. Stan Vincent, our centre forward, took big Jock literally and clattered into Sneddon near the halfway line. Stan's challenge couldn't have been called subtle.

At half time, Stein said to Stan, 'What was that all about? You're lucky that policeman at the players' tunnel didn't arrest you.' Stan was sitting in the corner and was muttering away under his breath. 'What are you saying?' shouted big Stein. 'Come on, spit it out.'

'It just doesn't matter what I do,' said Stan. 'I always do what you tell me but according to you, I can never do anything right.' I can't recall the manager's reply. Talking of Stan, he does a great job these days as the almoner for the Hibs Former Players Association. Stan goes out of his way to look after the wellbeing of any former Hibs players who are having a bit of difficulty. He wasn't a bad striker either as he got his fair share of goals.

When it comes down to it, there are only two strikers whom I can choose. They are of course Lawrie Reilly and Joe Baker. They were quicksilver, predatory and hungry for victory. They had that wee mean streak that all great players have and they were world class footballers. Lawrie and Joe would run defences ragged and score a barrowload of goals. Their styles would complement each other perfectly. One of the few occasions when they played together was in Lawrie's last game for Hibs. We beat Rangers 3–1 on the Monday night before the 1958 Cup Final against Clyde and Lawrie and Joe both scored. Make no mistake, they would form an unstoppable partnership. People might question their lack of height. Well, they shouldn't because Lawrie and Joe were both great in the air. Heading ability is about timing and having spring heels. Height is immaterial. Being small didn't stop Tostao or Gerd Muller from scoring headed goals. It didn't stop Lawrie Reilly or Joe Baker either.

I couldn't be happier with my front two. They would be more than a match for any defence in the world. In fact, any defender faced with the prospect of trying to keep Lawrie and Joe in check at the same time, would probably give the matter some thought then instantly retire from the game.

7

SUBSTITUTES OF SUBSTANCE

When I started playing, substitutes weren't allowed. When substitutions were introduced in the 1960s, each team was allowed to have one player on the bench. Over the years this has increased of course and we have now reached the point where seven subs are stripped and the manager can use any three of them. I think that this is just about right. It suits me fine to be able to name seven substitutes for my Hibernian Dream Team because I felt really bad about leaving some really top class players out of my original selection. The players I nominate to sit on my dream team bench will have mixed feelings. They will be pleased to have been named but they will be wondering why they aren't in the starting eleven.

I am going to surprise you right away by telling you that I am not going to pick a substitute goalkeeper. Hibs are a team based on attacking traditions and by doing without a back-up goalkeeper, I give myself the luxury of an extra creative player.

Peter Cormack came very closing to being selected in my actual team. He also almost made the substitute's bench. Peter started on the right wing, became a first class striker and finished off in the very best of company in the Liverpool midfield. Peter could also have solved any goalkeeping problems I had because he was excellent between the sticks as well. Peter exuded confidence and quality wherever he played and has missed inclusion in my squad by a whisker only because he is being compared with the very best of players.

So, I don't even have Peter as goalkeeping cover. This means that Alan Rough will just have to make sure that he doesn't get injured. He certainly wasn't one to miss too many games through injury in his playing days. I was at a fundraising event recently. Rough, Goram and Leighton were all there too. I was put on the spot and asked to name which of the three was the best Hibs goalkeeper. Before I could answer, Roughie intervened. He informed the company that there was no doubt that the best of the three was his good self. Alan never did lack confidence. That was part of the reason why he was so good.

I am only going to pick one defensive substitute. John Blackley gave Hibs great service for many years and was an outstanding player. John's best position was in central defence of course but, if he had to, I am sure that he could cover either full back position as well. Come to think of it, John would also be an ideal holding midfield player. I gave some thought to including big John McNamee. If we were facing a Kevin Kyle type, John would be the man to step off the bench and take care of him. I heard John described as a 'reducer' and a 'stiffener'. He could reduce the effectiveness of any centre forward by well and truly stiffening them, that's for sure. Unfortunately though I've had to leave Big Mac out because he only gives me one option. John Blackley was a better all round footballer and offers me more.

Someone not lacking in versatility is Des Bremner. Des began as a right back and impressed everyone when he stepped in to cover for John Brownlie after John broke his leg. When Des became a midfield player, he went on to greater things. He was capped by Scotland and was part of the Aston Villa team which won the English First Division and European Cup in successive seasons. Yes Des was good but not quite good enough to make my dream team bench I am afraid.

I was really disappointed that Bobby Johnstone didn't quite make my team. He will be among my substitutes and I am lucky to have him. My dad knew a good player when he saw one and Bobby Johnstone was his favourite player. My dad was a bit of a football connoisseur who admired classy players in all teams. Needless to say, he had a particular bias towards those who played for Hibernian. Bobby Johnstone didn't just succeed at Hibs. He was idolised at Manchester City and loved by the fans at Oldham. If he had received a bonus for every goal he created for Joe Baker during his second spell at Hibs, wee Bobby would have been a very rich man. Johnstone was a big success for Scotland too. He was good enough to grace any midfield and if he comes off the bench, he will certainly grace mine.

Alex Edwards can't be denied a place among my substitutes either. When I look at the very average players who represent Scotland these days and think that Alex never won a single full cap for his country, I can only shake my head in disbelief. Alex had plenty fire in his belly and that helped to make him the player he was. It also caused him to spend a lot of time sitting in the stand serving suspensions but without that fiery nature of his, Alex just wouldn't have been Alex. I have never seen a better passer of the ball. Alex's speciality was the cross field pass that drew the centre half into jumping for the header. Inevitably the ball would just clear his head and land at the feet of one of our forwards leaving him with time and space to score. A good example of this is the second goal in our 7–0 win at Tynecastle on New Year's Day 1973 (not that I need to remind anyone reading this book of that date, of course!). Alex's ball from the right took out the Hearts defender perfectly. Alan Gordon chested the ball down and fired it home for a copybook goal. Alex did this time and time again and as one of my subs, he has the opportunity to do it again for my dream team.

My next selection is Eric Stevenson. I had to think long and hard about leaving Eric out of the team proper. The fact that, in the end, it took George Best to keep Eric out, tells you just how good a player Stevie was. When I watched John Robertson of Nottingham Forest at his peak, he reminded me of Eric in the way that he shuffled up to defenders, swivelled his hips, changed gear and left them for dead. A killer cross and very often a goal would follow. Eric also reminded me of the great Stanley Matthews in that the defender knew what he was going to do but just couldn't stop him doing it because Eric's balance, quickness of thought and speed of movement were so good. Eric Stevenson wasn't quite George Best but he was certainly one of the best.

I've found a place for John Collins as well. I know that John saw himself as a central midfield player but to me he was three players in one. With his educated left foot and tackling skills, he was probably at his best playing left of centre in midfield. If we needed someone to play out wide on the left, John would give us extra back-up in that area and he could easily fill in at left back in an emergency. When a lot of his colleagues were heading for the pub or the betting shop, John took himself off to the gym. That dedication allied to his natural talent has won him a place on my dream team bench.

Neil Martin was a seriously underrated player. He's one of the best I've seen in the air and pretty deadly on the ground too. Neilly was a top striker. He is one of the elite band of players who have scored one hundred goals on both sides of the border and he combined pace, steel and a natural finisher's gift for goal scoring. Not many players go to

Parkhead and score a hat trick in a winning Hibs team but Neilly did just that. Martin could do a job in more than one position as well. He could perform well as an orthodox striker, support a main striker or drift in from out wide on the left. He played on the left when Scotland beat Italy at Hampden in the World Cup in 1965. Jock Stein managed Scotland that night and nobody will ever forget the casual but perfectly weighted pass with the outside of his left foot that Jim Baxter made to lay on a last minute winning goal for John Greig. Neilly would be the ideal impact sub. He would come on against tiring defenders, bully them and get you a vital goal just when you needed it.

My last sub is Jimmy O'Rourke – Mr Hibs himself. Jimmy and I were school mates and team mates. We've also been lifelong best mates. Jimmy would be great in the dressing room, competitive on the pitch and the source of an awful lot of goals. Why did I pick Jimmy? Just because he is Jimmy – an out and out Hibs man, a great player and my long time friend. It would be unthinkable for me to have a Hibernian Dream Team that didn't include Jimmy O'Rourke. He was always going to be in. He most certainly is in and my team is the better for his presence.

I now need a physio to keep my dream team players fit. A physio is a key role at a football club and the best of them can make a really big difference to a club's success. In my opinion, we had the best physio of the lot at Easter Road in Tom McNiven. Thomas Gray Anderson McNiven to give him his full title was ahead of his time. He was using technology to treat injuries long before others had even thought of such a thing. Some physios were over cautious and told players that they would be out for a few weeks. Tom was the opposite. He was always encouraging you to believe that you would be back in no time at all. His powers of persuasion and his healing skills inevitably had you back on the field much quicker that you had a right to expect.

Tom used to regale us with stories about his exploits in the Korean War. He would show us his medals too. We thought that he was a war hero until we found out that the medals were for running! Tom's athletic prowess was obvious when he took our fitness training. It was really enjoyable and gave us the edge in fitness over a lot of teams.

You could always confide in Tom and know that it would go no further. This was the opposite of some physios who would go running to the manager as soon as you left their treatment room. If Tom had seen you burning down the main stand, he wouldn't have told the manager.

Tom used to take private patients in the afternoon when the players had gone home. One day Jimmy O'Rourke and I had stayed on for some extra practice. As we were going along the corridor on our way out, we spotted three senior police officers disappearing into Tom's den. When they were in, Jimmy opened the door and shouted, 'Now remember. It's cash only and no receipts.' We ran down the corridor laughing.

Tom came out very angry and shouted after us, 'I'll see you two in the morning!' He swore at us and then realising what he had done went back into his room muttering, 'Sorry, Chief Inspector. I beg your pardon for that.'

Tom used to tell us that he hadn't been a great player. He had played junior football though for Stonehouse Violet. He always said that he had plenty of endeavour but no class. Well, he had class to spare as a physiotherapist. That is why he was made the Scotland physio and he combined that job with his duties at Easter Road. I've got the best of players in my dream team and I have the very best of physios to take care of them.

I need a chairman to work with my manager. Harry Swan

was still in the chair when I joined Hibs but I didn't have much to do with him. Mr Swan presided over one of the most successful periods in Hibs history and held high office in the Scottish Football Association. As a boy and a young man, I wasn't knowledgeable about Harry Swan's period at the Easter Road helm. For that reason, I have decided not to consider Mr Swan for the chairmanship of my Hibernian Dream Team. He sold the club to William Harrower not long after I arrived and I got to know the new chairman quite well. Mr Harrower was quiet, reserved but very, very astute. I liked him.

Tom Hart was next in line and he wasn't scared to spend his money. He made sure that Hibs had the best of everything. One small example of this was the way he fitted us players out for travelling. We were always smartly dressed in quality clothes. We looked smart and we felt good. I don't think that Mr Hart always spent his money wisely though. He lavished a fortune on Joe Harper when we didn't need him and recouped the money by selling Alex Cropley who we most certainly did need. Tom Hart also gave Eddie Turnbull too much power during his time as manager in my opinion. Allowing a manager free rein can be a recipe for trouble and in Hibs' case, it led to relegation and a spell in the doldrums.

When I was manager, Kenny Waugh was chairman. I liked Kenny and enjoyed working with him. I would have liked to have had more money to spend but it was a tough time at the club and I realised that.

Kenny Waugh's vice chairman was the late, great Kenny McLean. Kenny never became chairman of Hibs but was a hugely influential figure in our history. He was a highly friendly, popular man but, like all successful businessmen, he had an inner core of steel. When Wallace Mercer tried to take over Hibs, our club's very future was at risk. It really was as serious as that.

Kenny McLean stepped forward and, along with others, led and masterminded the successful Hands Off Hibs campaign, which played a large part in Hibs ultimate survival. Who could ever forget the rallies at Easter Road and the Usher Hall that Kenny organised? He stood on the stage at the second of these rallies and proclaimed that Hibernian would rise like a phoenix from the ashes. We did, and today, thanks to people like Sir Tom Farmer and Rod Petrie, we are stronger than ever.

So, great credit then goes to the much-missed Mr McLean. Hibernian Football Club will forever be in his debt.

When Kenny Waugh sold out to David Duff, very few of us had any idea what the next few years had in store. Duff originally splashed the cash and allowed Alex Miller to bring in some top notch players. He also did things like joining the fans on the terracing. I always wondered what that was all about.

Duff had plenty of get up and go but by the end of his reign our club had almost got up and gone. It was a big fright and a narrow escape and we were all relieved to see Tom Farmer, as he was then, bring some financial stability to the club.

Douglas Cromb took the chair for most of Alex Miller's managerial reign. To say he was close to Miller would be an understatement. He displayed blind loyalty to his manager and that wasn't a good thing. Hibs were not in a healthy state on the playing side when Alex resigned in 1996. Not long after Mr Cromb stepped down as chairman of Hibs, he assumed the chair at Raith Rovers. That surprised me, as I always thought that Hibs were his team.

Tom O'Malley's spell in the chairman's office was marked by his obvious love for our club. He also deserves great credit for the way in which he successfully steered Hibs to promotion during their season in the First Division.

Rod Petrie was appointed by Sir Tom and has proved to

be an inspired choice as both chairman and chief executive. A lot of fans think that Rod is too cautious and want him to release more money for signings. I have been guilty of that myself at times.

In fact, Rod Petrie has been an exemplary chairman. A decaying old ground has been replaced by a fine modern stadium which is now three quarters complete, with the final piece in the jigsaw, the new East Stand, already a work in progress. We have a state of the art training complex which is bought and paid for and our debt is much reduced. To achieve this, Rod Petrie has had to sell a lot of good players. This can't be avoided.

When a player knows he can get more money elsewhere, he will move and his club can do very little to stop him. I reckon we have taken in around £15 million in transfer fees in recent years and without that income our debt would be close to £20 million. That is just not feasible so the player sales had to take place.

Rod Petrie hasn't always got it right. Meeting a player deputation in John Collins' absence was a mistake. I am sure that Rod acted for the best of reasons. He probably felt that he could sort the matter out quickly and that by doing that he would save John having to get involved. As it turned out, things escalated, the press and media had a field day and John possibly felt less than fully supported.

Rod has generally supported his managers well. Alex McLeish, Tony Mowbray, John Collins, Mixu Paatelainen and John Hughes have all been given money to spend on players. Some of them have used that money more wisely than others but that is not the responsibility of the chairman.

A lot of people criticise Rod for being a bit serious and methodical. I've got no problem with that. If I want a laugh, I'll go to a comedy show. What I want in my chairman is reliability, financial acumen and a willingness to speculate sensibly.

Rod Petrie has all of these qualities and he is my choice to be chairman of my Hibernian Dream Team.

I'm now moving on to select my captain and my manager. No matter how good your team is, and mine is very special, you need top men in charge on and off the pitch. I will now analyse the candidates and decide on the right men to lead my dream team.

8

CAPTAINS COURAGEOUS

That's my Hibernian Dream Team squad in place. When I was manager at Hibs in the early eighties, it was really difficult some weeks to field a team that I was happy with. Our resources weren't great then and it could be a bit of a struggle to put together a quality combination. In selecting my dream team, I've had the opposite problem. It was a real challenge to choose just eleven players from a list of so many greats. It's been really hard having to leave out some tremendous players. Having said that, what a team I've ended up with. I've got a team that I'm really pleased with and a team that could take on and beat the world. My substitute's bench is pretty useful as well.

Now I need to pick my captain. I don't want someone who just runs out at the front of the team and tosses the coin. I want a skipper that the whole team will like and respect. He also needs to be able to inspire the team when the going gets tough and be strong enough to represent the players' views to the manager and chairman when issues come up.

Finding the right man shouldn't be a problem as Hibs have had some great captains over the years. Gordon Smith led the team during the Famous Five era and I am sure that every player at the club looked up to him. He was exemplary both as a player and a person. Gordon was a quiet, dignified man but he also possessed an inner strength. If Gordon was captain, no one would be in any doubt who was in charge.

Gordon was succeeded by Eddie Turnbull who had a different style of captaincy. Joe Baker used to say that Eddie was a shouter. Joe added, 'And when Eddie shouted, he really shouted.' When Joe recalled the game at Tynecastle when he scored four goals against Hearts as a seventeen year old, he would talk about Turnbull playing behind him that day and constantly being on his case. There was no chance of Joe resting on his laurels because Eddie kept driving him on to even greater efforts. Given Joe's success in that match and many others under Turnbull, Eddie's approach obviously worked with him. It might not have worked as well with every player though.

My first two skippers at Easter Road were John Fraser and Joe Davis. They were both well liked and respected by the rest of the team. They had no favourites and didn't make a fuss about being the captain but just got on with their job. They were both consistent performers and sure of their place in the team every week, which helps. They gave the other players sound advice but in a quiet friendly way. They were also positive, cheerful types and that strengthened their position in the dressing room.

I was asked by Bob Shankly to succeed Joe Davis and of course I was happy to do so. I considered it a tremendous honour to be given the opportunity to captain the club I loved. When Shankly offered me the captaincy I remember thinking back to supporting the club as a schoolboy and thinking how great it would be to play for the Hibs. Now I was going to be the captain and that meant an awful lot to me.

Bob Shankly wasn't one to let anybody's head get too big and after he had told me why he was making me captain and had listed the qualities which I would bring to the job, he finished up by saying, 'But just remember, you're no indispensable.'

One of the duties of captaincy of course is representing the players when they have a complaint which they want taken to the manager. In my early days in the job, I had an unusual problem to deal with. Hibs had just started providing lunch for the players at that time and they did a great job. The food was excellent. One day as I was finishing my meal, I heard footsteps coming towards my table. I looked up and saw that I was being approached by a deputation of first team players. I wondered what serious matter was needing to be addressed and got the shock of my life when they told me that they weren't happy with the meals. One day we would have chicken, the next steak and the day after that it would be fish. I didn't think that there was much to find fault with but I was wrong. My team mates were sure that the mashed potatoes we were being served were of the instant variety. I was told to go and see the manager and tell him that his players wanted 'real tatties'.

I went to see Bob Shankly. When I told him why I was there, he just stared at me. There was a silence for what seemed to me like half an hour. He then said, 'Tell me again because I cannae quite believe what I'm hearing.' When I repeated the players' complaint, he just shook his head and said, 'You can tell them that there will be no change.'

Most of my time as skipper I was able to concentrate on the footballing side of things. I had the privilege of leading Turnbull's Tornadoes. What a pleasure that was. The team was so talented and had so many strong personalities that it virtually captained itself. It is a source of great pride to me that these great players gave me their total respect and loyalty during my time as their captain.

One skill which I had to work on when I led the Tornadoes

was the art of lifting trophies. I did it three times in a year and it got better every time. To stand at Hampden holding aloft the Drybrough Cup or the League Cup was an unforgettable experience. I stood looking at the sea of Hibs scarves and banners below me and thought, 'This is what it's all about. This is what I came into the game for.' When I was a wee boy playing football in the streets imagining that I was playing for Hibs at Easter Road, that was what I had dreamed about; now my dream had come true.

Jimmy O'Rourke and I had discussed how we would celebrate at full time if we won the League Cup. At that time, the winning team wasn't able to do a lap of honour with the cup after it had been presented. Jimmy suggested that we should run to our fans before the presentation and I agreed. When the referee blew for time up, I remembered what Jimmy and I had discussed and gestured to the team to follow me down to the Hibs end. As we stood there with our hands aloft to acclaim the best supporters in the world and listened to their chants of 'Hibees, Hibees', I looked up at the terraces and thought if I wasn't standing down here, I would be up there among them.

Sometimes as captain, I would have to go and see Tom Hart the chairman about bonuses. Hart was usually pretty fair and he would normally agree to the requests that I took to him. If I was approaching him on behalf of a player he didn't like though, it was a different story. If the chairman thought that a player didn't fully respect what Hibs stood for and didn't give his all consistently in a green and white jersey, he would simply put his foot down and refuse to pay them what they were asking for.

After that it was up to the player to accept this or to look elsewhere for his livelihood. Most of the time though, we were well looked after at Easter Road.

My biggest regret as captain was not being able to lift the Scottish Cup. We thought that we had a great chance in 1972 but Celtic beat us 6–1. That score was totally flattering to them. It was a wide open game and we created a lot of chances. If we had taken them, it could have finished up 6–4 or 6–5. Unfortunately our finishing was poor and our defending was even worse. We were just too cranked up for that game and that stopped us from playing our normal game. We felt terrible for the fans that night and pretty bad for ourselves as well. I never did get the chance to return to Hampden as Hibs captain in a Scottish Cup Final.

When I moved to Celtic, my captain was Kenny Dalglish. Kenny had a cutting sense of humour and if he wasn't pleased with someone he would use this to put them down. Some players responded well to this but others were crushed by it.

George Stewart took my place as captain at Easter Road. George's love of Hibs shone out of him. His whole manner said to his team mates: 'This is Hibs. We are a great club and playing for us is something special. Let's go out and do the fans proud.' It's always good when a club is led by a man who buys into its culture completely. We certainly had that when George wore the armband. George brought a very positive approach to being skipper. When Hibs reached the Scotish Cup Final in 1979, we beat Hearts in the quarter final. In case any of the players were in any doubt of the outcome of that match, George told them before the start that playing Hearts was 'a walk in the park'. Hibs duly went out and won 2–1 and George got one of the goals to lead by example.

Jackie McNamara followed George as captain. Jackie was a natural leader with a forceful personality and very clear principles. It's no secret that Jackie had firmly held political views. He was never slow to express them and I respected that in him. When I was manager, Jackie would often come to me to represent the players and put his case strongly. He was always fair though and he always took the club's financial position at that time into account.

When Gordon Rae succeeded McNamara, it was obvious that he had learned from Jackie. This was to Gordon's credit as Jackie's approach had a lot to commend it. Gordon was no less definite in his views than Jackie but he was always prepared to keep an open mind in discussions. He brought an infectious enthusiasm to his captaincy and was particularly good at helping and supporting the younger players.

Alex Miller raised a few eyebrows when he appointed Andy Goram as captain. The relationship between Goram and Miller is an interesting one. Alex took life seriously and came over as a bit dour. Andy was the total opposite. He lived life to the full and couldn't have been more outgoing if he tried. Despite these differences, Miller signed Goram and made him his captain. Goram was a larger than life character who would have been a major presence in the dressing room. The players would have looked up to him because he was such a great goalkeeper.

Murdo McLeod was the man who had the honour of lifting the Skol Cup in 1991. The scenes that greeted the players when they brought that cup home to Leith were something none of us will ever forget. Murdo still talks about that experience and it obviously means a lot to him. He played a big part in the winning of that trophy and it was even more special because the club had been close to going out of existence only a year earlier.

I can still see Murdo and Alex Miller walking out on to the pitch at Easter Road when they came back to the stadium that night. They had their arms round each other as they held the cup up for the fans. It looked like they had the perfect bond between captain and manager. Only a short time later, Alex moved Murdo on. I was never sure why he did that. Maybe he thought that Murdo was a threat to his position as manager. We'll probably never know.

During his short spell in charge of the club, Jocky Scott brought John Hughes to Hibs and made him captain. That proved to be a very sound move. If you walked into a dressing room of sixteen players, it wouldn't take you long to pick out John as the leader among them. He was a natural. There would be something wrong with any player who couldn't get fired up for a game with John Hughes as his captain.

When Hibs went to Tynecastle for the Millennium derby, nobody gave them much of a chance. Their captain thought differently. He told his players in no uncertain terms what the game meant to Hibees and he made it clear to them that anybody who came back in after the game having failed to pull his weight would have his captain to reckon with. When John delivered this message to the team, his language might have been less than parliamentary at times but no one would have had any difficulty in catching his drift. Hibs achieved a famous victory that night, of course, and Yogi played a big part in that.

Just like John Hughes always seemed destined to captain Hibs, it also always seemed that he would return to the club as manager one day. That has now happened and it would be fitting if a born and bred Leither like John could end the Scottish Cup drought that we have all had to put up with for far too long. I'll tell you one thing. If John did bring the Scottish Cup home, Leith would be the place to be that night and for a few nights after that.

Franck Sauzée was an excellent captain for Hibs. Sadly, he struggled as manager. I don't think that his lack of total fluency in English helped him when he was in that role. He never struggled as captain though. Quite the reverse. On the field,

Franck was able to communicate with his feet and no one spoke the international language of football better. Players who didn't always give him the respect he deserved when he was in charge in the dressing room gave him total commitment when he was the leader on the pitch. Franck's pride in being captain of Hibs was there for all to see and the fans loved him for that.

Rob Jones was also a good captain for Hibs. He was an intelligent man and, like all the best captains, he led by example. Nothing summed that up better than his performance in the 2007 CIS League Cup Final. He definitely deserved to hold up the trophy at the end of that game.

Rob found himself in an awkward situation when, as captain, he got caught up in the stand-off between John Collins and his players. He also made it clear in his last season with us that he wanted to return to England for family reasons. The fans didn't hold these things against him though because they respected him as a man, a player and a captain. His commitment to Hibs' cause on the pitch was always complete and he will be fondly remembered at Easter Road.

Now I have to decide who the captain of my Hibernian Dream Team is going to be. It can't be just any skipper because the team of many talents that I have assembled would take a bit of commanding. They are all strong personalities so I need someone that they would all look up to.

They would all admire Willie Hamilton's ability but Willie wasn't really the captaincy type. He would make a good social convener though. Mind you if you put Willie in charge of the kitty, he would be last seen heading for George Street with George Best just behind him.

I don't want to put myself forward for captain of my dream team because I want to savour the experience of playing in it. Franck Sauzée could take the armband and he's a strong contender but I think that, really, there is only one man for the job. That man, of course, is Gordon Smith. Even in this team of all time greats, Gordon's playing ability would win him the respect of his colleagues. When you add this to his likeability and natural authority, the case for Gordon grows. We're not finished yet because Gordon has an established track record of success as Hibs captain. He led the club to three league titles. I don't think any Hibs captain will ever do that again.

Gordon's credentials are impressive. He was a great player, a great captain and a great Hibee. He just has to be my Dream Team captain and I am delighted to say that he is indeed the man who will lead my team.

9

THE MEN IN THE HOT SEAT

Great managers make great teams. It is as simple as that. You only need to look at Manchester United before Alex Ferguson took over and compare their record in that period with the club's success in the Fergie era. The facts speak for themselves. Similarly, Celtic struggled pre-Jock Stein and then won the league nine times in a row when he took over.

It goes without saying then that I want a top quality manager to take charge of my dream team. Just as I have been spoiled for choice with the players who have been at Easter Road over the years, I have an impressive group of managerial candidates to choose from as well.

Hugh Shaw was still Hibs manager when I signed provisional forms for the club. He was a distinguished figure with silver hair who was always in a lounge suit. I don't think that I ever saw Mr Shaw in a tracksuit. He had been an excellent player for Hibs and had also been the club's trainer. When Willie McCartney died suddenly, Shaw was promoted to the manager's office.

He had the nucleus of a great team around him and chose not to change it much. Hibs won the league three times in five years under his management and they did this with players who, in the main, had been brought to the club by McCartney. That is not to diminish what Hugh Shaw achieved. Having the players is one thing but getting the best out of them is something else again.

After I became a provisional signing at Easter Road, I would train there on a Tuesday and Thursday night. Eddie Turnbull was the trainer and after my first Tuesday session, he told me to go up to see the manager to get my expenses. I went up to Mr Shaw's office and he handed me a ten shilling note. The equivalent of ten shillings these days would be fifty pence but ten shillings would buy you a lot more in those days than fifty pence would now. I took that first ten bob note home to my dad and he never spent it. We kept it in the family as a memento of my first payment from Hibs and I still have it to this day.

When Hugh Shaw decided it was time to step down, Harry Swan appointed Walter Galbraith. Galbraith had matinee idol looks. He was like a Scottish version of Clark Gable. He had mainly played and managed in the lower leagues in England, so he was a bit of an unknown quantity when he came to Hibs. The chairman didn't give him too much money to spend and most of his early signings were free transfers from down south. None of these players were to prove great acquisitions.

He did sign me as a full professional though. For some reason, Hibs had been showing no urgency in offering me a full contract. When word started to go round that Chelsea and one or two other big clubs were showing an interest in me, they soon changed their tune. One day a sleek, white Jaguar pulled up outside our house in Niddrie. That caused quite a stir in our street, I can tell you. Walter Galbraith was the driver and it transpired that he had come to offer me a full professional contract. Although my dad was desperate for me to sign for Hibs, he didn't show this in his dealings with Galbraith. We were both a bit put out by the way Hibs had initially dragged their feet in approaching me and for a while we played hard to get. It was only a front though because there was only one team I wanted to play for and my signature was soon on the forms.

We hardly saw Walter Galbraith during the week and when we did, like Hugh Shaw before him, he was dressed in a suit. He would give us our team talk on a Saturday but looking back, none of what he said was particularly memorable and he didn't go into anything like the level of detail that managers go into today.

When William Harrower replaced Harry Swan as chairman, he made money available for Galbraith to spend and he put it to very good use. He made four signings: Pat Quinn, John Parke, Neil Martin and Willie Hamilton. I think that it's fair to say that given the right budget, Walter Galbraith had an eye for a player. He certainly gave me my first-team debut and I am grateful to him for that. We were playing Motherwell at Fir Park on the Saturday and during the week, I got a wee inkling that I might be in. Jimmy McColl had been a great goal scorer for Hibs before the Second World War and now, in the early sixties, he was still on the club's backroom staff. On the Thursday morning, Jimmy came over to me and said, 'You might be involved on Saturday so be ready.' He was right and I was in at inside left. I must have been ready because I scored, but we lost 4–3.

William Harrower was very rich but he was completely down to earth. He owned a chain of betting shops and drove a very impressive Rolls Royce. I think he was the last person at Easter Road to own a Rolls until we signed Stevie Archibald. Mr Harrower's main shop and personal office were in Queen Street. One day he turned up at the ground in a Vanden Plas Princess. It was a nice car but it wasn't in the same class as his Rolls Royce. I asked him why he had got rid of such an impressive car and he replied, 'Have you ever tried to park a Rolls Royce in Queen Street?'

Changing his car wasn't the only decision that the chairman made. He also changed his manager. Out went Walter Galbraith and in came Jock Stein. Everything altered at Easter Road for the better. We now saw the manager in a tracksuit every day and training was much more fun. We did less fitness work and far more ball work. Stein was a colossus of a man in every way. He was a big man with a big personality and a massive presence. Some managers have to work hard to get the players' respect. Stein commanded it naturally. When he walked into a room, everyone took notice. There was a real aura about him.

When he was introduced to the players, he made his mark right away. He told us, 'There are going to be changes around here but what these changes are will depend on you and not me.' What he meant of course was that he intended to take the club places and it was up to us if we wanted to be part of that journey. Believe you me, every one one of us wanted to go wherever this impressive, imposing figure standing in front of us would take us.

In those days, you hardly knew a lot of your team mates. You came in, did your training and went home. Stein changed all that. He took us on a pre-season trip to Newtonmore. When we were there, we trained, played golf and went for walks together in the beautiful countryside. All the time we were getting to know each other and friendships were forming. Nowadays, they would call it team bonding.

Even today a lot of managers are wary of the press and media. Stein was the opposite. He cultivated them. He reasoned that you normally paid a lot to advertise a product so if you could promote your football club for free through the back pages of the newspapers, why not do so. He had a network of journalistic contacts and he drip-fed them stories on a regular basis. That way, his club got maximum coverage and he controlled the content. It's fair to say that Big Jock was a shrewd operator.

He never gave you feedback right after a game. He always waited until the Monday morning. You had calmed down by then and you were better placed to take in the advice he gave you. It was usually simple but always effective. In one game, I had got annoyed at a referee's decision and kicked the ball away in anger. When I came in on Monday morning, Stein beckoned me over and said, 'What was that about on Saturday? You were lucky you didn't get booked. The next time the referee gives a bad decision against you, here's what you do. Pick the ball up and walk over to your opponent with it. When you reach him, drop it gently on the ground and then get yourself back into your position. That way you'll make the ref think that you're a sportsman, you'll rile your opponent while giving the rest of the team time to get organised and you won't get into trouble either.'

When we were playing against Real Madrid, the Big Man said to us in the dressing room before the game, 'They're really good at carving teams open with one-twos. Remember, one-twos only work if you let yourself be drawn to the ball. Stay focused and stay with your man.' Simple and logical it may have been but it worked and nobody had ever told us that before.

Jock was also a psychologist. When I was at Celtic we went to Easter Road needing to win to clinch the League Championship. We had a few more games left to play, so it was really just a matter of time before we won the title and defeat to Hibs wouldn't have been the end of the world. The manager must have sensed that some of us were thinking along those lines because he simply said, 'You know, you don't need to win here today to win the league.' He then walked out of the dressing room. We looked at each other in disbelief. Surely Stein wasn't telling us that he didn't mind whether we won or lost. That would have been totally alien to his nature. He didn't lose many games but when he did suffer a defeat, he was a terrible loser. The atmosphere would be funereal for days and you would be desperate to make sure that you kept winning in the future to avoid a repeat of the gloom that had surrounded the club. It began to dawn on us this day at Easter Road that what he was really saying was, 'You might not need to win but I want you to and expect you to do exactly that.' That made every one of us determined to win the match and lift the title, so we went out and won the game convincingly. It's fair to say that Big Jock was employing mind games before the phrase had even been invented.

Talking of bad losers, Alex Ferguson was, and no doubt still is, one of the worst. When I was at Aberdeen, we all stayed out of Alex's way for a day or two if the team had lost. This hatred of losing goes hand in hand with an addiction to winning and that's part of what makes the Steins and Fergusons great managers.

When we played Real Madrid, most journalists didn't give us a chance. One reporter in particular predicted a heavy defeat for us. When we were celebrating victory in the showers after the game, the Big Man dragged the unfortunate newspaperman into our dressing room. He said, 'Boys, there's somebody here who wants to apologise to you.' The poor man had no option but to eat humble pie. Maybe it served him right for writing us off in the first place.

Stein had many qualities but one of the most important was recognising a player's talents and using him in a way that allowed him to perform to his very best. Again, that sounds simple but it's not. Too many managers use players in the wrong positions or ask them to do something that they can't. Big Jock used to point to the opposition dressing room and say, 'It's not about what they can do, it's about what you can do.' His philosophy was that if you had good players and you allowed them to play to their strengths, you would win more often than not. He was dead right.

Jock Stein was a wise man. He may not have had educational qualifications but he was an honours graduate of the university of life. Like Alex Ferguson, football was his all-consuming passion. Everything else was secondary. When I joined Celtic in 1977, Stein was older and had been through a bad car crash. He had mellowed but he still had that aura and he was still a winner. We won the league and cup double that season and the Big Man's influence was immense.

He was an expert at finding the right words. Celtic had gone through a spell of having players sent off and booked and Jock wasn't happy. He told us all to cut it out or we would have him to answer to. He really laid it on the line. The referee that day was David Syme. His father Willie before him had also been a referee and I don't remember either of them doing the Hibs too many favours. During this match, David Syme certainly didn't give Celtic the benefit of any of his decisions. Stein was furious. At the end of the match he was waiting on the touchline for Syme. He cut a fearsome sight, I can tell you, and we all feared the worst. I wouldn't have liked to have been in Syme's shoes and I thought that it was ironic that, having told his team to improve their behaviour towards referees, big Stein was about to lose it with one of them. I should have known better. Big Jock waited until David Syme drew level with him, looked him straight in the eye and said with real feeling, 'Yer faither would have been proud of you.' It was perfect. The referee knew exactly what the Big Man meant but he could not possibly have taken offence at the actual words that were spoken. It was Jock Stein at his considerable best.

He had been a powerful and influential figure at Easter Road too. We had won the Summer Cup, beaten Rangers three times in one season and defeated Real Madrid. We were second in the league with games in hand and in the Scottish Cup semi final. One Saturday in March, we beat Rangers in the Scottish Cup quarter final and went home on a high. When we opened the next day's Sunday papers we were brought right down to earth by the news that our manager had left us to join Celtic. I think most of us accepted that he would go back to Parkhead at some stage but it had never entered my mind that we would lose our manager quite so suddenly. The news devastated the whole team and our season just faded into anticlimax. Stein went to Celtic and won the Scottish Cup two months later. He then went on to win the European Cup and take nine league titles in a row.

I could understand him leaving because he was always a Celtic man at heart but the timing of his move was terrible and I could never understand that side of it. When I was at Celtic, I asked him about it. He said that he went right away because Bob Shankly, who took his place, was desperate to get started at Hibs and he didn't want to stand in his way. Stein and Shankly were great friends and it was the Big Man who recommended Bob to our board. I am sure that Shankly was keen to get to Easter Road because we had a fine team and we were well placed to win two trophies. It suited Stein to go to Celtic right away though and their gain was very much our loss. We will never know what would have happened had Stein stayed with Hibs until the end of the season but like all Hibs supporters, I just wish that he had.

I liked Bob Shankly. He was a true football man. He loved

the game and knew it like the back of his hand. The players soon realised this and gave him total respect. Bob was a quiet man. He was happy on the training ground and at the match on a Saturday but the boardroom intrigue side of things wasn't for him. Managers like Clough, Stein and Ferguson revelled in their ability to handle their directors and run their club in their own way. Bob Shankly shied away from the machinations of the boardroom and concentrated on what happened on the pitch and the training field. He was essentially a private man with simple tastes who liked nothing better than being out on the training pitch with his players. He was the total opposite of his famous brother Bill the successful, high profile manager of Liverpool. Bill was garrulous and Bob was reserved. They had a telephone discussion most days. Bill would talk non-stop because that was what he liked to do. Bob was quite happy to sit and listen. Come to think of it, the arrangement probably suited both brothers perfectly.

Like Stein, Bob Shankly was teetotal. He did like his cigarettes though. His number two was Jimmy Stevenson who had also worked with Jock. If you wanted something to reach the ears of Shankly but you didn't fancy saying it to his face, then you said it in front of Jimmy. That way you could be guaranteed that it would go straight to the boss. It had been the same when Stein was in charge.

Bob Shankly built a good team. Our football was enjoyable to play and attractive to watch. We gave most teams a run for their money and in a different era, Bob might have won something. At that time though, Stein's Celtic side was all conquering. You weren't just competing against the best in Scotland. Celtic were also the best in Europe. Mind you Shankly did mastermind a famous victory over one of Europe's top teams. When we lost 4–1 to Napoli in Italy, nobody thought we had a chance in the second leg. Except our manager, that is. We had played well in the first leg and the score had flattered the Italians. Bob was unusually outspoken after this game and declared publicly that we would qualify.

In the lead up to the game, he didn't go overboard because that wasn't his style. He just kept telling us with complete certainty that we would win. After a while his belief started to get through to us and we started to think that we could create an upset. In the event, of course, we did. The impact of Bobby Duncan's early goal in that game shouldn't be underestimated. It fired us up and rocked Napoli. I don't think even Bob Shankly thought that we would win that game 5–0 but he was his usual canny self after the match. When the press asked him for a comment, he simply said, 'I knew we would win.'

Bob hated selling players but he was forced to let a few go at Easter Road. He lost players of the class of Neil Martin, Jim Scott and John McNamee. He chose to sell Willie Hamilton to Aston Villa. After Jock Stein had left, Willie had reverted to his former bad habits. Bob admired Willie as a player but unlike Stein, who was prepared to work with him to keep him on the straight and narrow, he considered that he was more trouble than he was worth. I didn't agree with that and I am sure that a lot of Hibs supporters were sorry to see such a great player leave the club when he was happy to stay.

Bob was growing increasingly unhappy about having to sell players that he did want to keep. When he had to let Colin Stein move to Ibrox, his frustration was clear for all to see. Mind you, having taken in £100,000 for Stein, Shankly signed Joe McBride for less than £20,000. That was a great bit of business because Joe was a much more prolific goal scorer for Hibs than Colin had been.

Bob Shankly's successor couldn't have been more different. Willie MacFarlane was a Hibs man through and through and a complete extrovert. Willie had some good ideas and he freshened things up when he first came in. The players liked him and he got off to a great start, beating both Hearts and Rangers away in his first few games. In no time at all he had us sitting at the top of the league.

Willie's problem was that he could be too outspoken for his own good. Some players and directors can take straight talking. Others don't like it. Willie was also reckless in some of his comments to the press and this could cause him problems. He declared that Hibs would win the league and we didn't. He also said that Peter Cormack wouldn't be moving but he did. Willie was initially popular with the fans but when you build expectations and then don't fulfil your promises, this can affect your standing with the supporters.

Willie made some good signings. Erich Schaedler and Arthur Duncan are two top players he brought in for very reasonable fees. By the time he left though, his early momentum hadn't been sustained. He went very suddenly. We were due to play Liverpool in the Fairs Cup on the Wednesday night and Willie resigned on the Tuesday. No satisfactory reason was ever given for his resignation. It was rumoured that Tom Hart had told Willie to leave a particular player out of his team for the Liverpool game and that Willie had refused. The only one who really knew the reason for Willie MacFarlane's departure was the man himself. I used to see Willie at the Hibs Former Players Association meetings until his unfortunate passing this March and I will miss his great company. I never asked him why he decided to leave Hibs in a hurry though. That was his business.

Tom Hart had brought Dave Ewing in from Manchester City as a coach and Dave stepped up to replace Willie. Dave was one of these people in the game who are cut out to be coaches rather than managers. He took the job on though and did his best. He was big and burly and had his own style of diplomacy. He told us one day that his office door was always open and that we should feel free to come and see him any time we were unhappy with any of his decisions. He then added that hopefully after a discussion, we would come round to his way of thinking. He finished by saying that if after a conversation we still didn't agree with him, he would take us out to the car park and 'sort us out'. As far as I know no one ever took Dave up on his invitation!

Dave is best remembered, of course, for his statement just before a Scottish Cup semi final declaring Rangers were rubbish. Jock Stein had been an expert at using the media to place pressure on our opponents. Dave's comment had the opposite effect. If Rangers really were rubbish, then we would be expected to beat them at Hampden. We didn't and Dave's assertion rebounded on him. I am sure that he said it with his tongue in his cheek and the media seized on it to grab a few headlines. Mind you we did have a good laugh about it in the dressing room when we first read what he had said.

We all felt that Dave Ewing wouldn't be with us for long. We thought that he was just keeping the seat warm for somebody else and so it proved. In the summer of 1971, Dave headed back south and Eddie Turnbull left Aberdeen to take over at Hibs.

Eddie inherited some good players. Of the team that came to be known as Turnbull's Tornadoes, all except Jim Herriot, Alex Edwards and Alan Gordon were already at the club when Eddie arrived. He made a big impression. His training was superb, with a lot of emphasis on ball work. In no time at all he had us playing great football. He could be brusque at times although on other occasions, usually when you least expected it, he could be jovial. There was no doubt that he knew the game though and these were exciting times at Easter Road.

We reached the 1972 Scottish Cup Final. We didn't expect an easy game against Celtic but we thought that we had a good chance of beating them. There was a real rivalry between Eddie and Jock Stein. Eddie reckoned that he had been a much superior player to Jock and he now intended to better him as a manager as well. Maybe that contributed to our build up to this final. I thought that it was too intense and that instead of going into the game in a relaxed frame of mind, we went into it feeling on edge. We froze on the day and lost by the embarrassing margin of 6–1. I can imagine how our supporters felt that day. We players didn't feel any better. We knew we had let our fans and ourselves down.

Quite often Eddie stepped up training before big matches. I knew where he was coming from. He had a huge desire to win and this was reflected in his level of preparation. Sometimes though, like the boxer who over trains and leaves his best in the gym, we went into some important matches feeling tired when we should have been at our freshest.

We had some good results against Stein's Celtic but overall they came out on top more often than not in their matches with us. We were on the wrong end of some heavy defeats at both Hampden and Parkhead.

We did bounce back from our Scottish Cup Final humiliation very quickly though. Having been hammered in May we were back at Hampden for the Drybrough Cup Final in August. Again Celtic and Jock Stein were in the opposite corner. This time, Eddie got it just right. We were excellent in the first half and after an hour we were 3–0 up. However, Celtic like the great team they were, came back to 3–3. We were relieved to hear the final whistle as all the momentum had been with them. When Eddie spoke to us before extra time, he was brilliant. He told us that we had outplayed Celtic once already that day and that we were more than capable of going out and doing the same in extra time. He was calm and convincing and gave us our confidence back. Jimmy O'Rourke and Arthur Duncan scored great goals and we won an epic match 5–3.

We were on a roll now and we returned to Hampden for the third time in eight months in December for the League Cup Final. Again our opponents were Celtic and again we won. Eddie brought us to a peak for this game and our perform-ance did him credit. We won 2–1 but it could easily have been 4–1 and that score line wouldn't have flattered us. It was a great feeling to run to our supporters at full time feeling that we had repaid them for the letdown of the Scottish Cup Final earlier that year.

A few weeks later we went to Tynecastle and beat Hearts 7–0. Eddie Turnbull had only been Hibs manager for eighteen months but he had already won two trophies and recorded a historic derby win over our great rivals. He had achieved all this by high quality, varied training, tactics that were ahead of their time, and by assembling an exciting team of many talents.

We felt great going into that match with Hearts. We had been on fire in the weeks leading up to the game and Jimmy O'Rourke had predicted that some team soon would be on the wrong end of a hammering. He was right twice over. First we beat Ayr 8–1 at Easter Road. Then we went to Hearts' backyard and completely demolished them. We were 5–0 up at half time and the atmosphere in the dressing room was euphoric. I remember John Fraser, who was one of our coaches, saying that this was the kind of thing that you dreamed about when you were a schoolboy. John said, 'It's unbelievable. Imagine sitting in the dressing room at Tynecastle on New Year's Day five goals up on the Hearts.'

At that point Eddie intervened. He told us, 'Don't even think of easing off. Don't give them an inch. Go out there and bury them because that's what they would do to you.' He was dead right. If any of us had been thinking that our work was done for the day, Eddie had put us right on that score.

Hearts came hard at us at the beginning of the second half but we were ready for them. We withstood their pressure and came back to score two more goals. I ran fifty yards and slipped the ball past Kenny Garland for the first. Just as I was congratulating myself on getting on the score sheet in a match that was destined to live in Hibs folklore forever, Jimmy O'Rourke arrived to knock the ball over the line. When we were running back to the centre, I said to Jimmy, 'That was going in.' He replied, 'I was just making sure.'

To me, that was the high point of Eddie Turnbull's management of Hibs. We lost John Brownlie with a broken leg in the next game against East Fife and Alex Edwards picked up a booking in the same game, which led to a harsh eight week suspension from the SFA. To make matters worse, Eddie dropped Jimmy O'Rourke for the next match at Tannadice. Jimmy was our top goal scorer and it made no sense for him to lose his place. He had scored seven goals in his previous six games and didn't deserve to be dropped. We lost to Dundee United and our season fizzled out after that. Jimmy didn't fully regain his place in the team until the following November. We missed his goals and his effervescent presence and to this day, I have no idea why Eddie Turnbull left him out.

We were in the European Cup Winners' Cup quarter final against Hajduk Split from what was then Yugoslavia. We fancied our chances of lifting the trophy. We were certainly a better team than Hajduk. We beat them 4–2 at Easter Road and conceded a late goal. That came back to haunt us in the second leg. The atmosphere in Split was intimidating but we should have been good enough to get through. We managed to lose 3–0 and we went out of a competition we should have won.

Eddie was incandescent after the game. He felt that we had lacked character and on that day he was right. He took a decision to remodel what was an outstanding team and in doing that he was most certainly not right.

Turnbull's Tornadoes had been together for less than two seasons. We had the potential to win a lot more and all we needed really was some fine-tuning. Eddie embarked on major surgery. After the League Cup Final in 1972, Tom Hart had forecast more success for Hibs and had stated that none of the Tornadoes would be leaving Easter Road. This was one prophecy that fell well short. By the time of the 1979 Scottish Cup Final, Arthur Duncan was the only player from that great team who was still at the club.

For most of Eddie Turnbull's time at Easter Road, he and Tom Hart were very close. As a result of this, Eddie's power at the club was almost absolute. That isn't healthy. A restraining word from the chairman to the manager might have kept the Tornadoes together a little longer but it wasn't to be. Jim Herriot went first as he was held responsible for the defeat in Hajduk.

Our manager liked to receive praise and many times he fully deserved it. In all my years playing for him though, I never heard Eddie Turnbull accept blame for anything that had gone wrong. He wasn't big on apologies either.

We did win the Drybrough Cup again in 1973. Almost inevitably our opponents were Celtic. That was our last success. After that game the exodus from Easter Road gathered pace. Over the next few years Jimmy O'Rourke left for St Johnstone, Alex Cropley went to Arsenal, John Brownlie and John Blackley moved to Newcastle, Alan Gordon was transferred to Dundee and Alex Edwards found himself heading for Arbroath.

There was no logic about some of Eddie's decisions. In 1973 he signed Ian Munro from St Mirren. Munro was an excellent player but he played in left midfield and we already had Alex Cropley. We guessed that Alex was going to be sold. In due course he was but Ian Munro didn't get the chance to become his permanent replacement because he went to Rangers in a swop deal for Ally Scott and Graham Fyfe. There is no doubt who got the better of that deal and it wasn't Hibs.

Erich Schaedler was also involved in an exchange deal. Erich went to Dundee and Bobby Hutchinson came to Easter Road. We lost an international full back and gained a journeyman striker. I wasn't exempt from all this transfer activity either. For some reason, Eddie went off me and started to leave me out of the team. He never did give me a reason for this. Eventually, I was offered the chance to move to Celtic with Jackie McNamara coming to Hibs. I didn't feel that I was wanted by the club at that time, so I moved to Parkhead.

When I went in to Easter Road to collect my boots, Tom McNiven and the players wished me all the best. The manager I had served so loyally never came near me. I thought that he might phone me later on to wish me well but I never did get a telephone call. I remember coming out of the club that I loved and had served as player and captain for thirteen seasons thinking, 'So much for loyalty. I know it's a hard game but it doesn't need to be that hard.'

To this day, I don't really know why Eddie Turnbull chose to turn something that was so good into something that was very poor indeed. Eddie's Tornadoes were magnificent. It was a privilege to play in such a team. We did win trophies but if we had been left together and added to, we could have won so much more. By the time Eddie left Hibs, the team was about to be relegated and the great players of his original team had been replaced by players like Rikki Fleming, Bobby Hutchinson, Duncan Lambie, Jim Brown, Rab Kilgour and Joe Ward. The whole thing was really sad and totally avoidable.

Willie Ormond replaced Eddie and made a successful start to winning promotion back to the Premier League. Unfortunately, Willie had to give up for health reasons and Bertie Auld took over. Willie Ormond was a quiet, friendly man who really knew the game. He did well as Scotland manager and presided over the most successful spell in St Johnstone's history. When you went to Muirton Park in those days, you knew you were in for a tough game. Players like Henry Hall and John Connolly were a handful for any team. One of Saints' unsung heroes was Buck McCarry. Buck was a seriously big and powerful man. One day in Perth, he brought me down. I jumped up and kicked him and the referee sent me off. After the game, I was walking down the corridor underneath the main stand. Buck McCarry was coming the other way. There was nobody else around and the corridor was too narrow for us to pass each other easily so one of us would have to give way. Buck was mountainous but I was determined not to be the one to back down. McCarry just kept striding towards me. It was like the Gunfight at the OK Corral. Eventually we both reached the halfway point. We eyeballed each other and I feared the worst. I wasn't going to take a backward step though. Suddenly Big Buck burst out laughing, ruffled my hair and said, 'You silly wee bugger!'

Bertie Auld took Hibs up and kept them up but the fans didn't like the way his team played football. Survival by itself isn't enough for Hibs fans. We like a bit of style and Bertie's team certainly wasn't providing that. Kenny Waugh contacted me and invited me to become manager of Hibs. I was in charge of Dunfermline at that time and under very little pressure. I was honoured to be asked to come home but I knew that we had a poor side and that there was very little money to spend at Easter Road at that time. However, I knew that I would accept the job. I couldn't turn Hibs down and I might never be offered the job again. I brought Jimmy O'Rourke and George Stewart with me and we gave it our best shot. We knew that we had problems when Jimmy, George and I, along with a couple of the other coaches, played some five-a-sides against our first team squad. We just kept winning and we were all nearly forty!

We were so short of quality players and money that we had to employ some desperate measures. We signed Graeme Harvey from Ormiston Primrose Junior team and put him straight into the first team. I met Malcolm Robertson at Waverley Station and found out that he wasn't with a club. The following Saturday Malcolm played against Motherwell and we won 1–0!

It was only the presence of excellent players like Jackie McNamara, Ralph Callachan and Gordon Rae that kept us up. Alan Rough made a huge difference when he joined us from Partick. We were starting to bring through talented young players like John Collins, Paul Kane, Mickey Weir, Gordon Hunter, Callum Milne, Kevin McKee and Eddie May. They were going to be good but they weren't quite ready.

I kept looking for light at the end of the tunnel but all I could see was another train racing towards us. We had too many ordinary players and there wasn't going to be a quick fix. I had given it my best shot and I had built a foundation for the future. I decided to resign and let someone else have a go. I would have loved to have been in charge at Easter Road at a time when we had players of the quality of the many great players who had been colleagues of mine in my playing days. It wasn't to be though. I was in the right place at the wrong time.

One feature of my time as manager was that I got into a bit of trouble with the SFA. That wasn't like me. As a player, I had had the usual occasional disciplinary problem but nothing to worry too much about. That changed when I became manager. I felt that we were on the receiving end of a lot of poor refereeing and I tried to get the officials to explain some of their decisions to me. They refused and threatened me with a yellow or red card if I continued the conversation. I was never anything other than polite and I never used bad language but still the referees would not engage in a reasonable discussion. I felt that was poor.

A couple of times I ended up in front of the SFA. It was like being in a kangaroo court. Everything was geared to defending the referee and you got the impression that turning up and stating your case, no matter how convincingly you did so, was a total waste of time. The SFA always went with the ref, which left me with feelings of frustration and injustice.

Round about the time that I resigned, I received another fine from the SFA. It was £400, which was a lot of money then, and in my opinion it was completely unjust. I refused to pay it and was told that I would not be able to take up another post in Scottish football until I presented the SFA with a cheque. I never did write that cheque. Principles are important to me and I knew that I had been harshly treated. I did what I believed was right and I stand by my actions to this day.

When I stepped down, my assistant was my old friend and team mate John Blackley. I told John that if he was offered the job, he should take it. I told him not to worry about me and just to do what was right for himself. John did get the job and made a good start. He was given money to spend and brought in Gordon Durie, Joe McBride, Stevie Cowan and Gordon Chisholm. They were all good players and John took Hibs to the 1985 League Cup Final where Alex Ferguson's Aberdeen were too good for us. Sadly, John didn't manage to sustain his bright start. In the summer of 1986, Gordon Durie was sold to Chelsea for around £400,000 and John used the money to make five signings. He brought in George McCluskey, Billy Kirkwood, Stuart Beedie, Willie Irvine and Mark Caughey. Only McCluskey turned out to be a good buy. The next season started badly for John and didn't really get any better. If he had stayed, he might have turned things round but he decided to walk away. This was typical of John. He put the club first and himself second. Unrest was growing among the fans and he decided to give them what a lot of them seemed to want.

Kenny Waugh took his time in appointing a new manager but eventually decided to go for Alex Miller. Miller came to Easter Road in late 1986 and was to stay for ten years and become one of Hibs' longest serving managers. I always thought that his time in charge fell into three periods. He struggled initially and his team played defensively. The Hibs fans didn't like this and he wasn't all that popular.

When David Duff bought Hibs from Kenny Waugh, he gave Alex a big enough transfer kitty to bring players like Andy Goram and Stevie Archibald to the club. The young players who had begun to come through under John and myself had now matured and joined Alex's new signings in what was an improving team. When Tom Farmer rescued us from the mess that Duff had got us into, Douglas Cromb took over as chairman and provided the funds for Alex to buy more of the 'quality players' that he was always talking about. Murdo McLeod, Keith Wright, Darren Jackson, Kevin McAllistair and Michael O'Neill all came in and did well. This middle period of Alex Miller's reign was highly successful and brought the club its first major trophy in nineteen years. We won the Skol League Cup in 1991 and reached the final again two years later. We also achieved some high league placings. Alex deserves great credit for what he achieved at this time. He might have achieved more if he had replaced players like Graeme Love, Joe Tortolano, David Farrell and Brian Hamilton who gave their all but weren't really good enough.

The significant sums of money Alex had to spend must have been a great help. It certainly beat signing strikers from the junior ranks or plucking wingers from railway platforms. Alex had a very strong relationship with his chairman. This gave him a lot of power within the club. In my opinion, too much power for a manager is not healthy. It didn't help Eddie Turnbull in the end and it did Alex Miller no favours in the final analysis either.

In his last couple of years in charge, things didn't go so well for Alex. We lost 7–0 at Ibrox, which didn't go down well with the fans, and the team seemed to be going backwards. It didn't matter what Alex did (and he didn't always get things right), his chairman would never criticise him. It's good for a working relationship to be comfortable but it's not so good when it becomes cosy.

Alex Miller's last signing was Ray Wilkins who was forty years old. Ray had been a great player but his best days were well behind him. I couldn't see why Alex signed him and in his debut, we ended up defending in depth to hold a 1–0 lead against Raith Rovers at home. It was like Alex's reign had come full circle. He resigned after that game. Alex had been in charge for too long and I'm sure that, in his heart of hearts, he knew that himself. Douglas Cromb was heart broken to see Alex go and couldn't bring himself to appoint a new permanent manager right away.

He made Jocky Scott manager for 'an indefinite period' instead. I played against Jocky a lot when he was at Aberdeen and Dundee and he was a top player. He was fast and tricky and not the sort of player you would imagine would go into management when he retired. Most managers were reliable defenders or hard working midfield players in their day. Jocky has had a long career in management and coaching though and, at the time of writing, he is still going strong.

His spell as Hibs boss lasted around three months. The fans weren't impressed by signings like Rab Shannon and Brian Grant but they were happier to see John Hughes being brought to the club.

Douglas Cromb dispensed with Jocky's services without any warning at the end of 1996 and appointed Jim Duffy. Jim arrived at the ground for his press conference in a helicopter. I remember seeing this on the news and thinking to myself, 'He might be arriving in a helicopter but he won't be leaving in one.' Jim's first game was the New Year derby at home to Hearts and we lost 4–0. Maybe that should have told us something. I just think that the Hibs job was too much for Jim. He signed far too many players from lower league teams. You don't create a successful premier league team by buying first division players and Jim was guilty of doing exactly that. You don't see Manchester United signing too many players from Rochdale or Hartlepool, do you?

Mind you, Jim's Hibs team started off the 1997–98 season like a house on fire. We were playing tremendous football with Chic Charnley as the main man. We were leading Rangers 3–1 at Easter Road and looking great but somehow we allowed them to come back and win 4–3. That was the turning point. It was all downhill for Jim from then on in. By the time he was sacked, the season was approaching its last lap and it looked like only a miracle would keep us up.

The man who was asked to perform that miracle was Alex McLeish. Big Alex was just making his mark in the Aberdeen first team when I was at Pittodrie. He was certainly to prove a great player with a lot of success for both club and country.

Alex had charisma from the word go. He also had a really good sense of humour. He could make people laugh and that is a quality that shouldn't be underestimated.

I remember one day when I was taking training at Aberdeen, Alex came out a little later than the rest of the squad. He didn't hurry himself to join us either. I took him to one side and told him that it wasn't on. Good timekeeping is important at a football club and I told Alex that I didn't want to see a repeat of his behaviour. I don't think he was too impressed but years later when he was manager, he told me that I had been right and that he now preached the same message to his own players.

Alex had a big reputation in the game and that standing helped him to attract players like Sauzée and Latapy to Hibs. They might not have come if a lesser light than big Alex had been in charge. McLeish did a great job for Hibs. When he arrived, he almost did work a miracle and keep us up. He wasted no time in bringing us back and did it in style. He won the First Division comfortably and didn't take us into the Premier League to consolidate or survive. For two or three seasons we were a really attractive team under Alex and he nearly won us the Scottish Cup in 2001.

He knew how to win derby games and after Alex Miller, that was a pleasant change. Alex McLeish's team outplayed Hearts at Tynecastle in the last derby of the twentieth century and he followed that up with the famous 6–2 win at Easter Road a year later. It has to be said that the Hibs board gave Alex tremendous backing. They even gave him £750,000 to sign Ulises De La Cruz, which was unheard of before or since.

I was sorry to see Alex McLeish go when Rangers came calling but I didn't grudge him his next career move. He did well at Ibrox and has had successful spells with Scotland and Birmingham since. The sentimental choice to replace Alex was

Franck Sauzée and that's whom the directors went for. If they had stopped and thought about it, they would have realised that by making Franck manager, they were depriving the team of its best player.

Franck was only in the hot seat for a short time and nobody could call his time in charge successful. He might have improved as time went on but the early signs were that he just wasn't cut out for management. I think that it's significant that it's around eight years since Franck left Hibs and he has never taken up another managerial post. Maybe his experience at Hibs has put him off or maybe it just helped him to realise that being a manager wasn't for him. It was sad to see Franck go because he had been such a great player and ambassador for Hibs but I think that Malcolm McPherson made the right decision. It can't have been easy for Malcolm to reverse his original decision to appoint Franck so quickly. I know that a lot of fans thought that he had been too hasty in taking action but I think that he was both courageous and correct.

Bobby Williamson came in when Franck left and he was a very different character to the man whose place he had taken. Franck was an idealist but Bobby was very much a pragmatist. Bobby had done brilliantly at Kilmarnock but it just didn't work out for him at Easter Road. He introduced the promising young players at the club at that time and although Brown, Riordan, O'Connor, Thomson and Whittaker did well for him, they were really just feeling their way at that point.

The press loved Bobby because he always had something to say. When he told journalists that Hibs fans who wanted entertainment should go to the cinema, it was probably a throwaway line and not meant to be taken seriously. Our supporters did take it seriously though and it wasn't well received. Bobby's results weren't great and after two seasons in charge, he left Hibs for Plymouth Argyle. I don't think that there were too many regrets on either side.

Nobody expected Tony Mowbray to replace Bobby Williamson and when he did, nobody was sure what to expect from him. Tony promised to play traditional Hibs football and he delivered on his promise. He arrived at a perfect time because the top class youngsters who had come through under Williamson were now ready to make an impact. He made some excellent signings in Dean Shiels, David Murphy, Guillaume Beuzelin, Ivan Sproule and Rob Jones. He didn't do quite so well when he brought in Simon Brown, Zibi Malkowski, Antonio Murray, Amadou Konte and Oumar Konde. His team was fun to watch though and entertained the fans. He also got some great results against the Old Firm.

Inheriting a young squad was ideal for Tony because the players were receptive to his ideas and his coaching and there were no dressing room cliques to cause problems for him. Not all managers are so lucky. When Alex Ferguson and I were at Aberdeen, there were a lot of players there who had played against Alex and hadn't liked his style. They set out to make life difficult for Alex and a weaker man might have wilted. Alex, being Alex, took it all in his stride and moved the troublemakers out.

One of Tony's faults initially was to approach all games in the same way. Sometimes you have to change your style for a particular game or even for a crucial period in a match. He let himself down by losing to Dundee United in the 2005 Scottish Cup semi final. The game was won at 1–0 and Hibs should have concentrated on keeping their lead. Instead, Tony went gung ho and we lost the game. I am sure he learned from that and has become a more mature manager. It didn't surprise me when Tony was given the Celtic job but it has surprised me that he has got off to a slow start at Parkhead.

During his time at Easter Road, Tony never made a secret of his desire to move on to what he considered to be bigger and better things. He also made it clear that he felt his best players should be looking to move to bigger clubs as soon as possible. You can say that he was just being realistic or honest but I think that it's one thing to think something and something else again to voice those thoughts in public. In my opinion, his views were disrespectful to a club of Hibs' stature.

I was happy to see John Collins being given the chance to follow Tony Mowbray. John's reign was short and eventful and I am still a little puzzled as to exactly what went on during his year at the club. John won the CIS Insurance League Cup with Tony's players but the credit for that goes to him and him alone. He was the man in charge and he has the winner's medal. His team lost a Scottish Cup semi final to Dunfermline that they should have won and that's a blot on John's record. His signings weren't good and in losing Kevin Thomson, Scott Brown, Ivan Sproule, Michael Stewart and Stephen Whittaker, while bringing in a lot of ordinary players, he did himself and the club no favours.

When I first started hearing rumours about disharmony in John's dressing room, I put it down to idle speculation. The rumours persisted though and then the whole affair came out into the open. The player unrest that obviously existed must have hurt John and it didn't help his attempts to build a winning team. What struck me at the time though was that not one of his players came out and endorsed him unreservedly, which made me wonder just what was happening. John left pretty abruptly. One day he was raving about the new training centre and the next day he was away. I thought that was a bit strange as well.

Mixu Paatelainen took John's place and was welcomed by

the supporters. The fans had liked Mixu and were happy to get behind him. He never seemed comfortable in the manager's chair at Easter Road though. He didn't look at ease in his dealings with the press and media. It was also hard to work out what his favoured formation was and some of his team selections were a bit baffling. Mixu's style of play was more direct than Tony's and John's had been and that didn't go down well with the fans.

The crowd never turned against Mixu but I think it's fair to say that most people didn't think that things were going to work out for him. He dug deep at the end of season 2008– 2009 to grind out a win at Tynecastle and draws against Rangers and Celtic. He then decided to resign. These respectable late season results allowed him to go with his head held high and I think that everyone was pleased about that.

John Hughes was the supporters' choice to replace Mixu and Rod Petrie obliged. John wears his heart on his sleeve and has never hidden his affection for our club. He served his apprenticeship with Falkirk and has joined Hibs at a time when he has experience, energy and enthusiasm all on his side. He is naturally gallus and is a journalist's dream. Every day's papers are full of quotes from John. That helps to promote the club but John needs to guard against saying too much. Sometimes it pays to say less in order to achieve more.

John's early signings, like Anthony Stokes and Liam Miller, are exactly the type of players who should be at Easter Road. They have excited the supporters and that's always a good thing. History lies in wait for every Hibs manager. It is nearly 108 years since we won the Scottish Cup and the manager who finally brings that trophy home will be an all time Hibernian hero. Maybe John Hughes will be that man. I would like to think so. I have a lot of time for John and nobody wishes him more success than me.

Now I have to make my choice for the manager of my Hibernian Dream Team. I have narrowed it down to two candidates. You won't be surprised when I tell you that the men in question are Jock Stein and Eddie Turnbull.

Jock and Eddie were both great managers. Eddie served Hibs with distinction as an outstanding player in what was probably the club's best ever team. He then enjoyed a tremendously successful start to his time as team manager. Turnbull's Tornadoes would definitely have given the Famous Five team a run for their money in a head to head match and there are those who think that they might even have come out on top.

Having produced such a supreme team, Eddie then broke it up. He's not a man who thinks that he is wrong too often but I suspect that even Eddie would now admit that he changed too much too soon when there wasn't really the need for him to do so. What is worse is that the changes that Eddie made severely weakened a team that had been really strong. Hibs under Eddie Turnbull went from challenging regularly for honours and sometimes winning them to being relegated in a few short years. That shouldn't have happened and Eddie must take responsibility for it.

Big Jock was only at Hibs for a year. He was consistently successful during that time and all the signs were that if he had stayed, Hibs would have gone on to lift major titles. Who knows, we might even have won the Scottish Cup.

In making my final choice, I have looked at all aspects of being an outstanding manager. First and foremost you have to sign good players and then get the best out of them. Both Turnbull and Stein did well in this regard although in Eddie's case, his ability to spot the right type of player seemed to desert him at times in his later years at Hibs. Stein brought in John McNamee and Joe Davis during his time with Hibs and nobody could quibble about their ability. Eddie's first signings were Jim Herriot, Alex Edwards and Alan Gordon. They were all top class players, especially Alex and Alan. Mind you, as I have said, Eddie's later signings weren't always of the same quality.

Top managers also need to be tactically astute and able to outthink their opposite numbers. Again, both my candidates were experts in this field. You couldn't fault either of them for tactical awareness. Players also like their boss to be good on the training field. Eddie and Jock were certainly that. Their training was varied, innovative and challenging. I enjoyed the sessions that both of these great managers gave us and I looked forward to coming into my work every day.

Another key aspect is man management. Eddie fell down in this department. His football skills were stronger than his interpersonal skills. He would let personal animosity get in the way of his judgement and leave players out of the team or move them out of the club for reasons that weren't always clear and seemed to have little to do with the player's ability to deliver on the park. I found this to my cost when Eddie turned against me and stopped picking me for the team.

To this day, I don't know why he did that or why he was happy to let me leave Easter Road. I still had a lot to offer as I showed when I helped Celtic to a league and cup double in my first season with them. Ironically, we won the league at Easter Road. I have to confess to a feeling of satisfaction when I went home that night. It wasn't because Celtic had beaten Hibs. Far from it, I am a Hibs man first and last. My feeling derived from making a point to Eddie Turnbull. He had declared me surplus to requirements and allowed me to leave the club I had spent my whole career playing for to that point, without a word of thanks or an expression of good wishes for the future. I admire Eddie as a football manager but I don't respect him as a man because of the way he treated me and others who deserved better. I think that it's fair to say that Eddie and I don't exchange Christmas cards. That won't get in the way of my choice of manager for my dream team though. That choice will be made solely on merit.

Jock Stein never let personal differences get in the way of his team selections. Jimmy Johnstone drove Jock mad at times with his carry on off the pitch but Jock kept Jimmy at Parkhead and got the very best out of him for many seasons. He also instilled undying loyalty into the wee wonder winger. I remember when I was playing for Scotland with Jimmy in the early seventies. Tommy Docherty was the manager and we were staying at Largs. We had to meet a curfew in the hotel each night and all of us did except Jimmy. Two nights before the game, he rolled in during the early hours of the morning very much the worse for wear. Not surprisingly, the Doc read Jimmy the riot act. When he finished, Jimmy drew himself up to his full five feet five and said, 'You cannae speak to me like that.'

'Yes I can,' said the Doc. 'I'm your manager.'

'Naw you're no,' said Jimmy. 'Jock Stein's ma manager.'

Big Stein enjoyed unbroken success during his time with Hibs and what he might have achieved if he had stayed longer doesn't bear thinking about for Hibs fans. When he went to Celtic, it was a hammer blow for our club.

Eddie Turnbull's early years in charge were magnificent. He built a great team which played wonderful football and won trophies but, and it's a big but, he broke that team up far too soon. He then presided over a decline in playing standards at Easter Road, which led to relegation.

Jock Stein was a Celtic man. We all know that. Eddie Turnbull is a genuine Hibs legend who has made a massive contribution to our club over many years. I am faced with a really difficult choice but having weighed up all the factors that I have covered in this chapter, I am going for Jock Stein.

Jock was the best Scottish football manager who ever lived until Alex Ferguson came on the scene. He managed Hibs and did so brilliantly; that makes him eligible to manage my Hibernian Dream Team. I have to go for him because his all round managerial qualities and his magnificent record of uninterrupted success over many years make him superior to Eddie Turnbull in my opinion.

10

A HIBERNIAN DREAM TEAM TO SAVOUR

The challenge of picking a Hibernian Dream Team from all the Hibs players I have played with or watched in my life-time really appealed to me. I knew that I would have an enjoyable trip down memory lane and that is exactly the way it has turned out. I have always thought that Hibs, despite their ups and downs over the years, had produced more than their fair share of top players. Writing this book has confirmed that I was right.

For example, consider this team for a moment instead of my final choices. The brilliant Andy Goram in goal would be protected by a back four of Bobby Duncan and Erich Schaedler at full back, with John McNamee and Jackie McNamara as central defenders. Bobby was looking like becoming a really exceptional full back until he broke his leg. He was great going forward, which was no surprise because he started his career as a striker. Erich's tackles rattled the bones, he would have run though a brick wall and he had football in him too. Big John's motto was, 'They shall not pass but if they do, they will come down!' He got goals from set pieces as well. Jackie was an accomplished and constructive defender who would organise the defence superbly.

Johnny McLeod would be on the right wing. He had pace and trickery and could use either foot. His international recognition and the excellent spells he had at Arsenal and Aston Villa tell us just how good he was. Willie Ormond would be on the left wing. Willie was a great wee winger with an educated left foot. He didn't use his right much but neither did Jim Baxter and Ferenc Puskás and they weren't bad players, were they? Willie made and scored a lot of goals for Hibs. He started off creating goals for Lawrie Reilly and finished by setting them up for Joe Baker.

Between Johnny and Willie would be Eddie Turnbull and Peter Cormack. Eddie would power the team with his strength, stamina and skills. He would find time for a few rocket shots as well and would be our penalty taker. Peter would do what he did for Liverpool at the height of his career. He would make interceptions, link the moves and keep the team flowing forward, chipping in with a few goals as well.

Up front would be Alan Gordon and Stevie Archibald. Alan and Stevie had similarities as players. They were all elegance and intelligence and made the game look easy. They would effortlessly ghost into scoring positions and convert a high percentage of their chances. They would complement each other perfectly.

The seven substitutes would be the safe and sure Jim Leighton in goal, Des Bremner to cover full back and midfield in his usual hard working, understated but totally effective way, and George Stewart to provide back up in central defence and to remind everyone regularly what it means to play for the Hibs. Peter Marinello and Arthur Duncan would offer two more excellent options as wide men, Russell Latapy would bring his silky skills to midfield and Derek Riordan would add his all round talent and the potential for vital goals to our combination of super subs.

The fact that this is my *second choice* dream team squad shows just how many quality players have graced the Easter

Road pitch over the last fifty years or so. I could easily select third and fourth choice teams that wouldn't be short on class either. Seeing how good my second choice squad is also brings home to me just how outstanding the players in my dream team squad are. Let me remind you of my final selection.

Pat Stanton's Hibernian Dream Team

Alan Rough

John Brownlie   Franck Sauzée   Pat Stanton   John Parke

Gordon Smith   Willie Hamilton   Alex Cropley   George Best
Captain

Joe Baker   Lawrie Reilly

Substitutes	John Blackley
	Bobby Johnstone
	Alex Edwards
	John Collins
	Eric Stevenson
	Neil Martin
	Jimmy O'Rourke
Manager	Jock Stein
Physiotherapist	Tom McNiven
Chairman and Chief Executive	Rod Petrie

It really is a team to savour. When I have been writing this book, I have taken my task of picking an all time great Hibs team very seriously. Throughout the whole process, I have tried to imagine my team actually taking the field and playing together. I have thought about the tremendous individual skills that they all possessed and would all display in a match. Because they are great players, I am confident that they would blend together and combine their different talents to devastating effect. They would work hard too because truly great players always do. They give you perspiration as well as inspiration.

My Hibernian Dream Team would be more than a match for any team. Alan Rough would revel in playing with such brilliant team mates. He would smile and play at his very best because the big games always brought the best out in Roughie. Roughie's best was awesome so I wouldn't expect my team to lose too many goals.

John Brownlie would surge forward and combine with Gordon Smith on the right flank. I thought that John's link up with Alex Edwards was too good to be bettered but his combination with Gordon might just surpass it. John Parke at left back would be his usual unflappable self. John would win his tackles, look up, pinpoint the best player to pass to and deliver the ball perfectly, setting the next flowing move in motion. Both Johns would be rock solid in defence as well.

Franck Sauzée and I would love playing together. We would see all the play in front of us and that would suit us perfectly. We would keep the back door firmly shut and look to move forward to join our attack. I would link up with Willie Hamilton and Alex Cropley and keep going to get on the end of a pass or a cross. Franck would switch the play and bring Smith or Best into the game with one of his trademark long passes. Franck would be on the free kicks as well.

168

Gordon and Bestie would be unplayable. They could both beat players for fun. Gordon's crossing was simply the best and both our wingers would score goals and plenty of them. Willie would weave his magic in midfield. He would entertain the crowd, tantalise his opponents, notch some of his virtuoso goals and love playing with Alex Cropley. Alex would get up and down the left flank. He would crunch into tackles in his usual style, dispatch long and short passes and make his irresistible runs into the other team's penalty area. Alex would balance Willie perfectly and he wouldn't be short of goals either.

Our team is brimming with goals. Of the players I have mentioned so far, only Alan Rough in goal and John Parke wouldn't be a regular source of goals. When we hit the front two, we're really in business on the goal front. Joe Baker and Lawrie Reilly are simply two of the most prolific scorers in football history. They were goal machines in green. Joe and Lawrie's goals per game ratio would match anyone's. It's a pleasure to have them in my team. With the level of service that they would receive, they would be unstoppable. They'd break every goal scoring record in the book.

In the dressing room and on the training pitch, we'd have Jock Stein coaching, coaxing and cajoling. He'd get the very best out of this special set of players and lead them to non-stop success. Big Jock would also keep Willie Hamilton and George Best on the straight and narrow – most of the time at least!

If my dream team really could come together, it would win everything. We'd win the SPL, League Cup, Scottish Cup (at last), Champions League and World Club Championship and score two hundred goals a season in doing it. We'd have to double or triple the capacity of Easter Road and it would still be sold out every week. We Hibs fans would wonder what was wrong because we'd have nothing to complain about.

I hope that you have nothing to complain about when you read this book. I hope too that you've enjoyed sharing my memories and that you understand my reasons for making my team selection. Mind you, I don't expect you to agree totally with my choice. My co-author Ted Brack and I had many a lengthy debate before I finalised my choices. I changed my mind a good few times along the way as well. Sometimes, when we finished our discussion, I still hadn't fully made my mind up and I had to go away and sleep on it. I am completely happy with my final choice though.

It's my wish that this book will encourage all Hibs fans to think back over their time watching our great club. Like me, you'll have a host of memories of joys and disappointments and like me, you'll have been privileged to watch some ultra talented players wearing the green and white of Hibernian. I'll be happy if my book stimulates discussions over a pint before and after matches or over a glass of wine round the dinner table. It might even lead to the odd debate during your tea break at work. You'll have your own idea of whom you would pick for your dream team and you'll be convinced that your choice is better than mine. It'll certainly be different from mine. Enjoy your team selection and good luck with making it.

As for me, I am just going to sit back, close my eyes and imagine the wonderful football that would be played by the soccer superstars who make up Pat Stanton's Hibernian Dream Team.